HOTEL ROANOKE

The Grand Old Lady on the Hill

DONLAN PIEDMONT, NELSON HARRIS, LISA FENDERSON & ANNE PIEDMONT

Authorized by the Virginia Tech Real Estate Foundation Inc.

THE
History
PRESS

Published by The History Press
Charleston, SC
www.historypress.com

Cover image courtesy of the Hotel Roanoke.

First published 2019

Manufactured in the United States

ISBN 9781467144834

Library of Congress Control Number: 2019947299

CONTENTS

The Palm Court, later Oval Room,
in 1947. *Courtesy of Special Collections,
University Libraries, Virginia Tech.*

FOREWORD

I have been given a daunting task—writing a new foreword to the book my father wrote in 1994. Newly retired from Norfolk Southern Railway in March 1993, Donlan Piedmont took on the job of writing this informal history of Hotel Roanoke. For him, it was a labor of love, as the Hotel held a special place in his heart. As you can read in his author's notes, it was the site of his first date with his future wife, Dorathy Brown. The Hotel remained for them—and for my sisters, brother and me—a family favorite. Like many Roanoke families, we looked to the Hotel for special dinners. As children, we dressed in our fanciest clothes and used our best manners for dinner in the grand dining room. One sister had her wedding reception in the Pine Room (not a pub at the time), and another is a frequent guest when her Alexandria-based Virginia Tech job brings her back to the area. We may not be wearing our fanciest dresses, but I promise we do use our best table manners at dinner!

We have left Dad's narrative intact and have used many of the same photos that appeared in the original book. Where some are no longer relevant or available, we have substituted new ones. And, as this is an update or continuation of the Hotel's story, we have added some contemporary photos. Many of the names mentioned in the original have, like my father, passed on or retired. New players have picked up where they left off as the Hotel continues to adapt and thrive.

Dad closed the original book with a challenge: "The story of financing, construction and reopening of the Hotel has its share of disappointment, perseverance and triumph, and deserves to be told at a future time." The Virginia Tech Foundation, Lisa Fenderson of Blue Ridge PBS, Brian Wells of the Hotel Roanoke, Nelson Harris and I have picked up that challenge.

—ANNE PIEDMONT
April 2019

PREFACE

"Would you like to have dinner at the Hotel?"

For a young Roanoker growing up during the Great Depression, that meant more than dinner at the Hotel Roanoke. It meant nearly heaven. In a time of austerity, it meant opulence. In a time of scarcity, it meant abundance. In a time of drabness, it meant beauty. Hotel Roanoke, on a high hill, smacked of another world. Dinner at the Hotel? Who wouldn't want to go to Camelot?

Looking down on the emerging sooty city and the rail lines that were its lifeblood, the Hotel was formal while our lives were functional. We built with pine, but the Hotel used polished English walnut and carved oak. We had naked light bulbs—the Hotel had chandeliers. And wonder of wonders—could you believe it—a light went on automatically when you opened the closets!

I was born not far from the Hotel, though I didn't go there often. Still, it loomed large in my mind, as do castles and cathedrals for Europeans. Roanoke was the Magic City, and this was the spot where magic was turned into reality.

The Hotel was born with the city in 1882, when a lonely spot once inhabited largely by deer seeking salt at Big Lick set out to be a railroad boomtown. The railroad came, and so did the Viscose plant, which we proudly called "the largest silk mill in the world." The British-owned Viscose hired many officials (including my father) from England. Was it not right, then, that Hotel Roanoke should be built in the Tudor style? Didn't King Charles II call Virginia his Old Dominion?

The service, the accommodations and the food were exceptional. The landmark dishes gave Donlan Piedmont the original title of this book—*Peanut Soup and Spoonbread*—and he preserves both recipes in Appendix B. Try them.

But what can never be reproduced in today's styrofoam and plastic world is the ambiance, the sense of splendor, almost of wonder that we once felt when we entered. There was the great chandelier, bedecked with its pineapple, the symbol of hospitality; the lobby paneled in black walnut; the black marble tables; the Chinese sideboard; and portraits of our two Virginia demigods, General Washington and General Lee. There was the Writing Room, the Oval Room and the Crystal Ballroom, green, red and gold. This was somehow not only beautiful but sacred space.

And the murals! So far as I know, they were our only public ones. They were sentimental, unhistorical and wonderful: John Smith marrying Pocahontas, Patrick Henry captivating the assembly, the plantation thriving. Here was mythic Virginia, where the birds warbled sweet in the springtime.

God was in that heaven, and all was right with the world.

No wonder the rich and famous came here: John D. Rockefeller, J.P. Morgan (who liked the scrambled eggs), Jack Dempsey, Jeanette MacDonald, Dwight Eisenhower, Richard Nixon, George Bush and many more. This book demonstrates how a building can be one of the keys to the social and cultural life of our country.

One social event that I shall always remember was the *Gone with the Wind* ball held at the Hotel when that movie came out in 1939, a bonanza for the local American Theater. I was too young to go and hear the music (was it by the Roanoke Machine Shops Orchestra?), but I recall pictures of the local dandies, peacock-proud, dressed like Rhett Butlers, their gold

The lobby in the 1950s. *Courtesy of Special Collections, University Libraries, Virginia Tech.*

Snow scene, 1958. *Courtesy of N&W Photo, K.L. Miller Collection.*

chains dangling as they walked. No wonder the local Scarlett O'Haras waited with bated breath as their fans fluttered.

Far away in Europe, the world waited as Hitler invaded Poland and set off World War II, unlike any Washington or Lee could have imagined. Like many young Virginians, I left for that war from the N&W station, just across from the Hotel Roanoke. It was a cold night, and I was joining the navy. My father gave me a pair of long red woolen underwear, bought at nearby Oak Hall's. He had been to sea, and he knew I would need them. I did. As my train pulled out of the station, I looked at the Hotel on the hill. I carried that flickering view with me throughout the war.

In the postwar years, the Hotel grew old, like those of us who had admired it for decades, and as Donlan Piedmont tells us, it seemed doomed for death. Not so. This is a tale of revival and renewal. The Hotel Roanoke story is a story worth telling, and it is told well. Find out now for yourself.

Hotel Moribundis

One day toward the end of November 1989, a man, whose name, alas, is not known, came up to the front door of Hotel Roanoke, plugged his electric drill into a long

Early pictures of the Hotel, late 1880s; *top to bottom*: bleak, bleaker, bleakest.
Top to bottom: courtesy of N&W Photo, K.L. Miller Collection; courtesy of the Historical
Society of Western Virginia; courtesy of N&W Photo, K.L. Miller Collection.

extension cord and efficiently began to make history. In minutes—twenty possibly, thirty at the most—he had installed a sturdy lock on the right-hand door, just above the shiny brass plate. For the first time in its 107-year history, the stately, cherished old Hotel Roanoke had taken steps to keep people out.

Thus, the whine and whirr of an electrical device supplied a shrill lamentation to accompany the Hotel's last days. The unthinkable had occurred, and the old place, carrying its gentle burden of tradition and fame and glories, would in a few days go out of business. It would not—indeed, could not—disappear from the tribal memory of the city that for more than a century lay under its gaze.

—MARSHALL FISHWICK, PhD
Professor of Humanities and Communications Studies
Virginia Tech

AUTHOR'S NOTES AND ACKNOWLEDGEMENTS

During an airborne mission behind enemy lines in New Guinea in the Second World War, Bill Gearhart, Roanoker, and his commander, a lieutenant colonel in the Australian army, took advantage of a rare idle moment.

"Well, lieutenant," the Australian asked, "where in the States do you come from?"

"Virginia, sir."

"I have been in Virginia. What city?"

"Roanoke, sir."

"Ah, Roanoke, the place with that lovely hotel."

"The place with that lovely hotel"…invoked in a steamy green hell thousands of miles from the recalled elegance and charm of the Roanoke landmark.

Carter Burgess, distinguished citizen, once said that he was one of those Roanokers "who had never been south of Winston-Salem or north of New York until the war. I've been all over the world many times since then, and just about everywhere I went, I heard something about Hotel Roanoke from people who had wonderful memories of the place."

Such was the nature of the far-flung reputation of Roanoke's "Grand Old Lady on the Hill," a place that, from its beginnings in 1882, was the focus of the city's social and cultural life. The city and the Hotel, virtually founded together, were bound up in an indefinable almost mystical symbiosis, each drawing nourishment and growth from the other. The Hotel brought visitors to the city—famous and otherwise, such disparate personalities as Nelson Rockefeller and Billy Sunday, J.P. Morgan and William Jennings Bryan, Richard Nixon and Alben Barkley, Amelia Earheart and Van

Cliburn—and gave employment to generations of Roanoke citizens, most of them black. (It is a cruel and poignant fact of history that the Hotel had been flourishing for eighty-two years before black people could come into it through the front door instead of the employee entrance and order dinner instead of serve it.)

It was a part of Roanoke's life, the Hotel was, and mine too. My first date with Dorathy Brown was in its Fountain Room of happy memory. Less than a year later, we were in the Pine Room for our wedding reception. Marie and Richard Dunlap and Libbe and William Hubard and Sara and Jack Airheart, all Roanokers, spent part of their honeymoons there (one night costing the Airhearts ten dollars plus a fifty-cent tax and a three-dollar restaurant charge). Catherine Blair Fisher remembers that it was in the Regency Room that she had her first champagne cocktail. There were weddings, christenings and even a funeral, when the ashes of a frequent and long-staying guest were scattered on the grounds. There were dances, parties and conventions, and the Hotel moved to a national and even, as we have seen, an international reputation.

It produced Chef Fred Brown's peanut soup, Ken Wilkey's Whistle Stop, Fred Walker's and Carl Thurston's Virginia Night, Peter Kipp's Ad Lib Club, Janet Jenkins's thirty-year career of steady devotion, Doreen Hamilton Fishwick's valedictory and, for all who even once passed through its corridors, fond memories and nostalgia in bulk.

The Hotel was sustained by its railroad owner through the storms and calms of a hundred years; funds were always forthcoming, perhaps reluctantly but always generously and sometimes bravely, as when it made a significant investment for a major expansion in the Depression year of 1931. It became a corporate jewel to be polished and admired; it was a "club without dues," said one patron, "a club without membership," according to another. It was a place for lunch, a place for a drink, a place to meet friends, a place to make deals, smooth paths, settle civic matters. It dominated the city as socially as it did topographically, with its view of downtown just across the railroad tracks from its little hill.

The Hotel enjoyed a generally sunny passage through its 107 years, though dark clouds did occasionally cast shadows over it. A principal one was the employee strike that began at dinner on the night of October 1, 1983, and ended six months later in April 1984. The issues were wages and working conditions. Management, facing a competitive crunch, sought ways to reduce full-time employment and keep wage increases to a minimum. Called at home when the walkout took place, Peter Kipp and his wife went immediately to the Regency Room. With other management personnel, the Kipps waited on the tables, demonstrating in an odd sort of way the Hotel's unwavering commitment to service. Replacements were hired, and a large meeting scheduled two days later was handled without incident.

My aim in writing this work is not to produce the definitive history of Hotel Roanoke but to try to define and parse its reputation and character, hoping at least to suggest its rich tradition, its warmth, its people and the affectionate hold it exerted on so many—an affection that has continued even beyond the day it closed, November 30, 1989. I have learned that those who worked there, those who stayed there and those who perhaps only passed it by all looked on it with awe, affection, joy, disappointment and sadness, the whole range of human experience. I accept the burden of all of this book's flaws and omissions; but if, after reading it, people who have known the Hotel can say, "Yes, that's the way it was," or "I remember that!" and those who have never set foot inside the place can say, "What a wonderful place it must have been!" then I am more than willing to declare myself satisfied.

Deserving a large measure of whatever success that may attach to this effort, but totally exempt from its failures, are many, many people who gave their time and wisdom with kindness and patience. I cannot assign priorities of gratitude, but I am especially indebted to Janet Jenkins, retired general manager (described by several different persons as "a great lady"), for her memories and insights of the place that meant so much to her, and to three other former general managers of Hotel Roanoke—Doreen Hamilton Fishwick (its last), Peter Kipp and Fred Walker—who have been to me generosity personified. Thanks, too, to these former Hotel employees: Vickie Stump Cutting, Bruce Coffey, Lynn Schumacher, Mark Lambert, "Billy" Davis, Alphonso "Alex" Alexander, Warren Webb and Heinz Schlagel. My thanks go as well to Clare White, a historian of formidable talent and broad knowledge of the early days of Roanoke, and Dr. Nancy Connelly, executive director, both of the Roanoke Valley History Museum; to the staff of the Special Collections at the Carol Newman Library at Virginia Tech, especially Laura Katz Smith, to Belinda Harris of the library of the *Roanoke Times & World News*, to Carol Tuckwiller of the Virginia Room of the Roanoke City Public Library and to Ken Miller.

Providing both information and insights from Norfolk and Western Railway and Norfolk Southern Corporation were John P. Fishwick,

Dorathy and Donlan Piedmont's wedding reception, Pine Room, 1954.
Courtesy Anne Piedmont.

who was called from retirement by the late chairman of Norfolk Southern, Robert Claytor, to oversee Hotel operations, and who with Arnold B. McKinnon presided over its donation to the Virginia Tech Foundation; Richard F. Dunlap, Lawrence Forbes, William B. Bales, Reggie Short, Larry Keoughan, Arnold McKinnon, John Turbyfill, Richard Parker, Don Middleton, George Ruff, Frank Wilner (later a vice president of the Association of American Railroads) and Ann Fox Sprague (one-time assistant editor of the *Norfolk and Western Magazine*). Invaluable, too, were Roanoke city manager Bob Herbert, retired banker Dave Caudill and Virginia Tech's vice president Minnis Ridenour, who, with John Fishwick, supplied facts and background to the long and complex negotiations that culminated in the offer of the Hotel to Virginia Tech and its acceptance and the agreement of the city to build a conference center in connection with the Hotel.

Among individuals who helped me in one way or another are, in no particular order, Carter Burgess, Michael Ramsey, Senator John Warner, Senator Charles Robb, former congressman James Olin, Robert Garland, Ray Garland, Austin Neal, Kitty Fisher, John Vaughan, Margaret Baker, Elizabeth Bowles, William McClung, Charles Lunsford, Helen Fitzpatrick, Henry Hewitt, Betty Carr Muse, Mona Black, Ann Hammersley, John Eure, Sara and Jack Airheart and many, many more. They gave substance to this work and encouragement to its author by a word, a reference, a memory or two. I tender special thanks to Michael Ramsey and Bill McClung (retired public affairs director of Appalachian Power Company and an old boss of mine), who were both kind enough to read portions of the manuscript and offer constructive comments and suggestions, some of which I accepted. Also, Virginia Tech's Mary C. Holliman brought keen editorial judgment to these pages, to my benefit. With pleasure and thanks I acknowledge also Dr. Raymond D. Smoot Jr. and Mode A. Johnson of the Virginia Tech Foundation. It was their idea, based on a book about Washington's Willard Hotel, to produce an informal history of Hotel Roanoke; it was they who invited me to write it; and it was they who gave me encouragement and support every word of the way. With me were Dianne Smith, the book's talented designer, and Bruce Muncy, who contributed original photography for the book and other work on the project. To those I have listed and to those I may have overlooked go my thanks for bringing life and flavor to the rambling heap of stone, brick and wood known as Hotel Roanoke.

Feci quod potui, meliora potentes.

—DONLAN PIEDMONT
Roanoke
Winter 1993–Summer 1994

Chapter 1

HOW THEY BROUGHT THE GOOD NEWS FROM LEXINGTON TO BIG LICK

Halfway between Appomattox and the twentieth century, Big Lick, Virginia, in 1881 was an unremarkable place. The 1880 census listed 669 persons and about one hundred houses, fairly evenly divided between black and white residents. It had but one important business street, and that one unpaved and punctuated with steppingstones as crossings. Chartered as a town in 1874, Big Lick had a newspaper (the *Roanoke Leader*) and a railroad (the Atlantic, Mississippi & Ohio, the ambitiously named and at the time virtually bankrupt creation of General William Mahone). The town's principal industry seems to have been based on tobacco, for there were six factories, one producing cigars. This place with the unsophisticated name lay between Hollins College to the north and Roanoke College to the west, even then long-established and highly regarded institutions.

Great events involving the railroad were in the process of fruition, and the visionaries of Big Lick were quick to see the possibilities. Frederick J. Kimball, president of the Shenandoah Valley Railroad, and himself a world-class visionary, was looking for an appropriate spot where his north–south SVRR could cross the east–west line of the AM&O. The AM&O was bought for $8,505,000 by the same Philadelphia interests that owned the SVRR, and the owners quickly combined the two into the Norfolk and Western Railroad. In time, Kimball would serve as the NW's president on two separate occasions and was responsible for opening up the Pocahontas coalfields to Norfolk and Western traffic. That was yet to come, however.

The proposed intersection of the two railroads was hardly confidential, for surveyors were already busy looking at various routes in the Roanoke Valley. Aware of this, and sensing major possibilities for their town, the Big Lick establishment

Top: Inside view of a ballroom. *Courtesy of N&W Photo, K.L. Miller Collection*; *bottom*: the "English Beer Garden" in 1934. *Courtesy of Special Collections, University Libraries, Virginia Tech*; *opposite*: the staircase from the lobby, photographed perhaps in the 1920s. *Courtesy of N&W Photo, K.L. Miller Collection*.

assembled what was surely one of the first industrial development packages of incentives, offering land and cash (either $5,000 or $ 10,000—there are two versions from which to choose) to the railroad to locate in Big Lick. It was delivered on April 21, 1881, via overnight horseback rides by C.W. Thomas from Big Lick to Buchanan and John C. Moomaw from Buchanan to Lexington, where the Shenandoah Valley Railroad Board was meeting. The package and its rather golden evidence of Big Lick's interest had, according to Mayor Henry Trout (quoted in E.F. Striplin's *The Norfolk and Western: A History*), "a very good effect....Mr. Kimball remarked that the people of Big Lick were alive and at Big Lick the Shenandoah would have good friends."

His mind thus made up, Kimball—whom Roanokers subsequently and with good reason hailed as the man "to whom we owe so much"—saw immediately that Big Lick could not possibly absorb the enormous enterprise he was about to put in place there. Big Lick's eagerness was not enough. What was needed to complement a new and major railroad, a general office, a large machine shop complex was a new and major city.

He took the first step in that direction after turning down an offer to rename the town after him. "Call it Roanoke," he is supposed to have said. And he put the town's new name to an immediate and promising use by creating the Roanoke Land and Improvement Company early in 1881. Its goal was to build the city he foresaw would be essential to shelter and sustain the thousands who would flock to Roanoke to share the new prosperity that the railroad would bring. From the old Atlantic, Mississippi & Ohio would come 170; from the old Shenandoah Valley Railroad, another 200. Train service people from Lynchburg would add an additional 700, and the shops would add 100 more at first, with many hundreds more to follow. It was a lot of people to absorb, but Roanoke Land and Improvement Company was nothing if not optimistic—and prepared.

By 1881, the company held options on several hundred acres, acquired rather cheaply before the decision to set up headquarters was announced, and planned to acquire more. And not only to acquire the land, but to lay out on it streets for residences, commercial establishments and the machine shops where the railroad could repair and even build its own cars and locomotives (particular classes of which were described a century later as the "finest steam locomotives ever built"). Soon, the company organized water and gas utilities.

Roanoke Land and Improvement Company published advertisements in the *Roanoke Leader* for the sale of building lots "for all purposes." Looking ahead, the company declared that "the rapid development of the town renders this a particularly desirable point for store-keepers and mechanics to locate" and predicted that the railroad's shops "will give employment to 1000 mechanics," an ambitious but not impossible figure, as things turned out. For buyers of the lots, there were "very reasonable terms."

And so there were. Lots 25 by 90 feet cost $350; 70 by 130 feet, $600 (although some were tagged at $750). Lots on "hilly land" could be bought for as little as $100. The railroad sold lots to builders and contracted with builders for houses on its own lots for railroad officials. In November 1881, in a letter to Kimball, H.L Moore, an active builder in those heady days, reported the need for "the several streets of Roanoke 926 shade trees, placing ten trees to every block of 400 feet on each side of the street." Striplin writes that "between February 1881 and June 1882, the N&W or its subsidiaries erected 78 frame and 60 brick houses, and individuals, on lots bought from the company, erected a mill, two office buildings, 15 stores and seven dwelling houses."

P.L. Terry, one of the town's leaders and a subscriber to the fund that played a part in luring the railroad, advertised in the *Leader* that he had for sale "on the Installment Plan or for Cash, twelve newly built, nicely finished and well-arranged houses with eight and ten rooms in each." Installment payments would be "$40 per month and no interest," an arrangement difficult to resist. He also advertised "Fifty Choice Building Lots" in the neighborhood through which Jefferson Street ran and "where several of our best citizens have already located."

In the same period, Striplin notes, the number of Roanoke blacksmiths increased from three to seven, doctors from four to ten, lawyers from two to six and saloons from two to twelve. One new church brought the city's total to six, and the number of dwellings for the faithful and heathen alike increased from 58 to 268. In spite of the secular growth, "the single jail still sufficed." He observed also that the number of hotels had grown from three to nine.

One of those nine was Hotel Roanoke. Its forthcoming construction was signaled in the land company's original prospectus of February 1881: "And also to build and equip a hotel—capacity about 20 rooms." Thus, Hotel Roanoke was not a corporate afterthought decided on to ride the crest of a boomtown wave but an integral element in the town's development plan. Kimball himself selected the site in a wheat field on a hill north of the city and above the railroad tracks. City fathers, though pleased at the prospect of a new and almost-certain-to-be-grand hotel, would have preferred it to be elsewhere. Clare White, in her invaluable book *Roanoke 1740–1982*, quotes Mayor Henry Trout, who had been with Kimball on that fateful occasion: "I afterward reported to our people…what I had heard. They immediately appointed me a committee of one to go and see Mr. Kimball and ask him not to put the hotel and depot there, as we were afraid it would draw the trade off Franklin Road." The measure of his persuasive skills has been on view for well over a century.

The site settled on, work moved apace. George T. Pearson, 427 Walnut Street, Philadelphia, was the architect, his name printed with elaborate swashes on the list of construction specifications he had prepared. The design called for a Queen Anne building 177 feet long by 73 feet wide, and this had not been completed before an "annex" 132 feet long by 43 feet wide was attached. Its cost, $12,000, brought the bill for the entire project to about $60,000. There were to be thirty-four guest rooms in the original building instead of the twenty alluded to in the prospectus, plus thirty-five more in the annex.

Pearson's specifications are worth examining. He insisted, in adjective-rich imperatives, that all work was to be performed in a "true, perfect and thoroughly workmanlike manner" and with "good, proper and sufficient materials." Floor joists were to be three by twelve inches, cellar girders twelve by twelve, all sturdy timber and all yellow pine. The porch ceilings were to have two coats of linseed oil and "cleaned of all pencil marks and other defects; all hard wood work to be finished with Berry's Hand Oil Finish."

Brass bolts were to be installed on all inside doors and iron on all entrance doors. Speaking tubes were to run from the office to the kitchen and to servants' rooms. Kitchen specifications called for a seven-foot "French oven," two fires, two ovens and a thirty-six-inch wrought-iron furnace. An eighteen-inch portable furnace, made of "Russia iron," was installed in the bar.

Partitions in the privies were to be made of "beaded boards and the rooms lined with same; doors to be slat panel with spring hinges; seats to be 1-1/2 inches thick." These facilities were to be served by the first sewer line built in Roanoke, which ran from the Hotel and emptied into Lick Run, east of the building.

In May 1882, with construction already in progress, Roanoke Land and Improvement awarded a contract for one million bricks to G.H. Adams and Bros., of Lynchburg.

The bricks—$9^{1}/_{2}$ inches long, $4^{1}/_{2}$ inches wide and $2^{7}/_{8}$ inches thick—were to be manufactured in Roanoke, part by hand, part by machine. They were to be delivered to the site at the rate of forty thousand each week, and the contract price was $8.50 per thousand. A million bricks are a great many bricks indeed, far more, one would think, than the number required for what was essentially a wooden structure. Possibly Roanoke Land and Improvement, taking advantage of what was later called "economies of scale," bought them for later use in the construction of brick residences mentioned earlier.

There exists in the pages of the *Roanoke Leader* a thorough if breathless description of Hotel Roanoke as it stood in October 1882. It had begun receiving guests that

OPPOSITE   South wing, circa 1920s. *Courtesy of N&W Photo, K.L. Miller Collection.*

The Hotel in 1910, displaying a huge flag; *opposite, top*: a typical guest room of the late teens–early 1920s; *opposite, bottom*: the Dining Room, 1937. *All courtesy of N&W Photo, K.L. Miller Collection.*

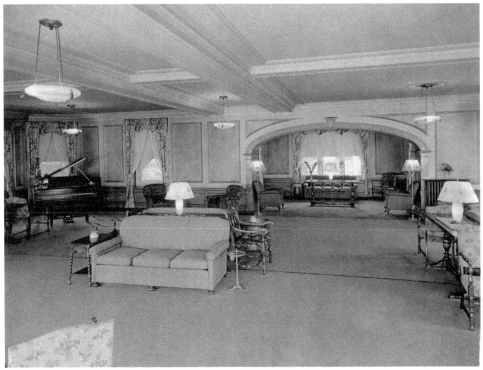

Opposite, top: The aptly named Sun Room, 1910; *opposite, bottom*: seating area, date unknown; *this page, top*: the airy Green Room of 1932; *this page, bottom*: the Colonial Room, formerly the Palm Court, later the Oval Room, in 1947. *All courtesy of N&W Photo, K.L. Miller Collection.*

same month, although the official opening was not to take place until Christmas Day. The writer was escorted on the tour by "H. Chapman, Esq, the polite and attentive superintendent of the Roanoke Land and Improvement Company."

In the basement was a barbershop "with bathrooms attached, all fully equipped and supplied with hot and cold water and finished up in handsome style." Next to the barbershop was a furnace room with a hot-air furnace "of large capacity" supported by three coal rooms, each thirty by forty feet. Sharing the basement space were "large, finely finished bar rooms, in which we observed large fireplaces of pressed brick after the Queen Anne style, which is the architectural style of the entire building." The basement also housed essential hotel functions, a steam laundry and the bakery, with an eight-by-six-foot oven.

The dining room—"saloon" in the vocabulary of the 1880s—was "extremely handsome" and could seat two hundred under six chandeliers of eight lights each. Like the office and public parts of the building, the dining room was finished in hand-rubbed and polished English walnut, carved oak, cherry and ash. The dining room was served by a butler's pantry (with "electric and speaking tube connections") and a kitchen "completely equipped with all appliances and aids to the culinary art." The range consisted of two fireboxes, three large ovens and an "immense broiler and boiler of great size." A dozen floor-to-ceiling closets housed the china and were "fitted up with apparatus for warming dishes."

The new Hotel sought to offer elegance along with up-to-date conveniences. All guest rooms featured hot and cold running water, and many had zinc or porcelain bathtubs, said to be among the first in Roanoke, at least, where one could bathe in a "warm and private place." An interconnected and complicated system of bells and speaking tubes permitted guests to direct their various wishes to the staff. By means of a small ebony knob in the room, the guest could call a bellboy (one ring), chambermaid (two rings), ice water (three rings) or hot water (four rings). An elevator ran to the third floor from the basement, and for those who chose not to put their trust in the system of ropes and pulleys that supplied its motive power, there was "a grand stair ornamented with carved and polished oak and lighted by a handsome stained glass window."

The attentive Mr. Chapman told the writer that five hundred trees had been ordered for the grounds, which were being graded at the time and would be lighted by nearly

OPPOSITE Three views accenting certain forgotten features of the Hotel of the past. *Top to bottom*, an odd little tower facing the west, date unknown. *Courtesy of N&W Photo, K.L. Miller Collection*; cheerful striped awnings, facing south, 1920. *Courtesy of Special Collections, University Libraries, Virginia Tech*; and the verandas, shaded with vines, probably photographed in the teens. *Courtesy of Special Collections, University Libraries, Virginia Tech.*

This gate led to the Hotel from the corner
of Shenandoah Avenue and Jefferson
Street, or somewhere close to it. *Courtesy of
the Historical Society of Western Virginia.*

two dozen gas lamps. The mention of such a large number of trees might have been puffery on the part of the Roanoke Land and Improvement superintendent, for there is no evidence that such a forest ever graced the ten-acre site.

"Taken in its entirety," the Hotel was, the *Leader* concluded, "one of the most commodious, well arranged, and handsomely finished hotels we have ever seen outside of a few of our largest cities. There is one feature, however, in which it cannot be excelled, and that is the magnificent view presented from the verandas and every window and door in the building. The view needs to be seen to be appreciated. We have neither the ability nor space to depict it in words. On every hand the horizon is met by mountains of attractive outline, while the landscape intervening is beautiful and attractive....This cannot fail to become a most popular resort, and under the experienced management of the lessee, Mr. Mullin, will soon become famous with the traveling public and visitors to our growing city."

This Mr. Mullin is a shadowy figure. His name does not appear in the accustomed references about the Hotel. In its fiftieth anniversary edition (November 30, 1936), the *Roanoke Times* says the first manager was George L. Jacoby, succeeded in 1888 by Fred Foster. Foster was also the manager of smaller hotels the railroad owned in Bluefield, West Virginia, and Pulaski, Virginia. Between 1893 and 1901, the manager was S.K. Campbell, replaced in the latter year by Foster again; and when Foster died, his widow assumed the managership. Subsequent managers will be catalogued in appropriate places as this narrative proceeds.

An 1882 photograph of the completed Hotel Roanoke shows it stark and rather bleak, landscaped with a few bushes here and there and no sign of the five hundred trees Mr. Chapman had promised. The Hotel's half-timber, half-stucco appearance it retained all its life was clearly established. The "annex" formed one leg of a right angle, parallel to the railroad tracks. Its roof, pierced by dormers, sloped gently down to protect covered verandas, already partially concealed by vines, running the length of the building on both floors. The other leg of the building faced Jefferson Street and seemed to be all gables, projections, more porches and even the suggestion of a gambrel roof. Guests entered the grounds through a gate at the corner of Jefferson Street and Shenandoah Avenue driveway and followed a sweeping path to the entrance, located approximately at the point where the two legs of the angle met.

It was through that entrance that Roanokers flocked in 1882 to celebrate with Christmas dinner the formal opening of the Hotel. For a new hotel in a community whose rough edges had not yet been smoothed down, it was a haute monde event. There were nine courses on the menu:

Merry Christmas

SOUPS
Chicken à la reine
Consommé

BOILED
Turkey, celery sauce
Mutton, à la sauce

COLD DISHES
Boned Turkey en aspic
Ham
Chicken Salad
Lobster Salad

ENTREES
Filet de Boeuf pique aux
    champignons
Petit Pate of Oyster
Lobster
Diamondback Terrapin a la
    St. Cloud
Timbale of Macaroni a la Nelson

ROAST
Rib of Beef
Turkey and Cranberry Sauce
Young Pig
Goose and Applesauce

VEGETABLES
Mashed Potatoes
Green Peas
Sweet Potatoes
Tomatoes
Corn

PASTRY
English Plum Pudding,
    Brandy Sauce
Apple Pie
Mince Pie
Peach Pie
Lemon Meringue Pie

DESSERT
Pound Cake
Fruit Cake
English Wafers
French Kisses
Lady Fingers
Vanilla Ice Cream
Wine Jelly

FRUITS
Figs
Oranges
Bananas
Malaga Grapes
Raisins

Pecans
Almonds
English Walnuts

Coffee
Chocolate
Tea
Cheese

The price attached to this sumptuous bill of fare is unknown, but it surely included the costs of bringing the more exotic foods into Roanoke by train from more sophisticated centers like Washington, Richmond or possibly even New York. More important than the cost was the clear identification of the new Hotel as the center of elegance and hospitality in the new city and the source of pleasure and profit for the Hotel.

Few could have known it, but with that dinner, the Hotel Roanoke mystique and tradition began, and the second knot in the silken rope that eventually bound the Hotel and the city together was tied just a year or so after the official opening.

Roanoke's young bloods, newcomers to the town with the railroad and its associated activities and restless for a social life, had begun to look to the Hotel Roanoke as its locus and beyond the city limits for much of their companionship. They organized the German Club, arranged for its first dance and invited dates from more or less nearby cities and counties. Accompanied by their chaperones, the young women came— by rail, on reduced-fare tickets—and "were installed at the Hotel Roanoke…at the expense of the local swains."

This opening "German" was subsequently described in the columns of the *Leader* as "the most brilliant and recherché society event that has yet occurred in our city." Since Roanoke was only just emerging from its wooden sidewalk stage, this claim, in truth, could hardly have meant much.

The festivities began at nine o'clock to the "sweet strains" of the Roanoke Machine Shops Orchestra. By then, "the parlors were thronged with the beauty and fashion of our city, supplemented by charming representatives from different portions of the state as well as abroad. All were in full evening costume, the somber dress suits of the men contrasting prettily with the warm colors of the ladies' costumes.…The ballroom was handsomely decorated, brilliantly illuminated and seemed to mirror the happiness and pleasure so clearly expressed in the face of each participant in the many and intricate figures."

No doubt, but such happiness and pleasure were of necessity confined to the dance floor and the parlors, and not mirrored elsewhere. For Number 12 in the club's bylaws for 1883 stated unambiguously that "members shall not be allowed to go upon the second floor of the Hotel during the evening of a German, but must leave their partners at the first landing of the stairs, where they will be met by a maid especially appointed for that purpose." Some years, the revels continued the next day with a "morning German" that ended only when the imports and their chaperones took the train home.

In the 1880s and '90s, the Germans were formal affairs, featuring mostly the "graceful, stately waltz," although there was a generous sprinkling of polkas and

gavottes as well. In the decades that followed, the dance program, abandoning the gavottes, reflected the fads and tastes of the day: the frug, bunny hug, jitterbug, turkey trot, foxtrot, Charleston, conga, samba, rumba and others, some now as forgotten as the sarabande and as passé as the minuet.

In the earlier days, decorations were "simple in the handsome ballroom of the Hotel Roanoke, but the dances were gay and brilliant functions." Orchestras might come from Richmond, favors from New York, refreshments from Philadelphia. In later years, there were five Germans each season: Opening, Thanksgiving, New Year's, Mid-winters and Easter.

Very likely many of the same musicians who made up the Roanoke Machine Works Orchestra also played in its band, which in the early days of the twentieth century

ABOVE Helen and Broaddus Chewning, parents of Helen Chewning Fitzpatrick, costumed for one of the traditional "Germans." *Courtesy of Eric Fitzpatrick.*

OPPOSITE In the 1938 remodeling, the ceiling of the Oval Room required eighteen coats of dark blue paint. *Courtesy of Special Collections, University Libraries, Virginia Tech.*

gave afternoon concerts on the Hotel lawn. The appearance of the grounds had been steadily improving from the bare, stark look following the building's completion. The effect was due to the energy of a man named Patrick Foy. A friend of Kimball's, he supervised the building of a stone wall around the property (where parts of it remain in place to this day), undertook major plantings of trees and flower beds and built at the Hotel the first greenhouse in the city. Foy cared strongly about that greenhouse. On September 16, 1890, he wrote a penciled note to a Mr. Churchill of the Norfolk and Western Railroad's Engineering Department. "From all appearances, we are going to have an early fall," he wrote, adding diffidently, "I think it would be well to make some Provisions for the Heating of the Green House as soon as possible." Then with a touch of asperity, he finished, "There is also some 6 glass [window panes] Broken which ought to be repaired at once and the doors can hardly be Shut from the way they are Swelled." It was signed, "Yours Truly, Pat Foy."

Generous with the railroad's funds when it came to the greenhouse, he was careful, even frugal, when it came to himself. His expense account for the month of August 1890 (submitted on buff stationery with "Hotel Roanoke, Roanoke, Virginia, Fred E. Foster, Manager," printed ornately in blue) totaled nine dollars. It covered four days in Bluefield, two in Lynchburg and one in Pulaski.

He died at the age of eighty in 1924, one of the last links of the Hotel to its origins. (But not the last. That distinction belongs to J. Ed Brown, headwaiter, who joined the Hotel staff in 1882 and sixty-two years later was still on the job and making a good thing out of autographing the Regency Room menu featuring his photograph.)

Through all of this, the tradition of the German continued. From time to time, there was a variation from the traditional black- (or even white-) tie events. Helen Fitzpatrick of Roanoke remembers "when mama and papa used to dress in costume to attend the German Club Masquerade Balls at the Hotel." Austin Neal, who was the club president in 1934, remembers going to one of the Masquerades as a Spaniard—"a blond Spaniard"—with trousers tucked into high boots and a white shirt with big sleeves.

At the Germans during Prohibition years, he recalls, the band would be playing away cheerfully, but the dance floor was empty. "They were all off somewhere drinking." This was a significant departure from the Victorian rectitude that had installed By-law No. 12, which in any case had by that time been repealed. Once, a heavy snow made it impossible for Neal and his wife, Betty, to leave after the dance, so they spent the night at the Hotel and returned home the next morning still wearing their evening clothes, "an interesting sight for the neighbors."

(Another of Neal's memorable experiences with the Hotel involves a high school banquet in 1926. "At the end," he recalled, "there was this little coffee spoon by my

plate. So I put it in my pocket as a sort of souvenir. The next morning, my father saw it on my dresser, and there was an uncomfortable conversation with him. He told me I had to take it back, that it wasn't mine to have. Since he worked in the railroad offices across the street, I asked him if he wouldn't take it back for me. 'No. You took it. You return it,' he said. So I went in to the lobby, thinking that everyone there recognized me as the well-known spoon thief. I laid that spoon on the registration desk and ran out.")

The first duty of the German Club's new president was to make arrangements for the next season's dances. "I called on Ken Hyde or George Denison to fix the dates

ABOVE Roanoke City aerial featuring Hotel Roanoke sometime after the 1938 renovation. *Courtesy of Virginia Room, Roanoke Public Libraries.*

and with Charles Hofer to arrange the menus," Neal said later, invoking three of the great names in the Hotel's pantheon. "Being president was not an arduous chore."

Long before Neal's adventures in the Hotel, patronage was steadily growing, and for good reason. The Hotel was becoming established as more than a place to spend a night, especially for families. It sought to carve a niche in the resort market, which in the latter part of the century was a growing one. Well-to-do-families left the summer heat of the cities in search of fresh mountain air, relaxation and all the spiritual refreshment that flows from the proximity of pristine nature. Hotel Roanoke had just that combination, as a promotional brochure from 1885—just three years after the Hotel opened—made clear, plus its own elegance. It had become "a most delightful resort, not only during the summer months, but throughout the year. It has a cuisine acceptable to the most fastidious and affords every comfort to be found at home. [It is] within reach of the Natural Bridge, Peaks of Otter and other attractive places, to which delightful excursions can be made." Guests ever since have made the same "delightful excursions."

Not too much later, the Roanoke Chamber of Commerce had this to say in a promotional piece of its own:

> *Although for the past year her capabilities for entertainment have been often put to the test, the city is well provided. The pioneer of the large hotels is Hotel Roanoke, owned by the Norfolk and Western Railroad Company and located opposite the depot upon an elevation which makes it a prominent object from any approach. The architecture is of a cottage-like character, with an abundance of piazza space. It is not too much to say that broad porches, clad with Virginia Creeper, form one of the most restful and agreeable spots in the entire city. There are few hotels north or south affording a more beautiful outlook. At the present time a large and costly addition is being built on the western side, and when this is done, the "Roanoke" will contain 150 bedrooms and will have a frontage to the south of 300 feet. It is under the management of Mr. Fred E. Foster, who also had charge of the Norfolk and Western Railway's "Inns" at Radford, Pulaski and Bluefield.*

An unidentified patron about this time wrote about the Hotel in terms that have since been widely quoted. It was "a splendid hotel crowning the hill in the midst of lawns, parterres of flowers and ceaseless fountains....The parlor is as pretty a room as you will find in many a mile, and the dining room light and cheerful....The table and service are of a high order...and I do not know a better resting place...between Philadelphia and Florida."

Norfolk and Western trains entered the city, bringing passengers from all points, foreign and domestic, attracted to the Hotel by such persuasive and seductive rhetoric.

The Shenandoah Valley line had connections through Hagerstown to cities of the Northeast, including especially New York. The main line ran from Norfolk, with steamer connections to European and Atlantic ports. Guests from the south came by rail from connections at Winston-Salem, Durham and Bristol and from Washington via Lynchburg. Porters met these trains and escorted passenger-guests out of the station, across the street and up a shady path that led to the Hotel's inviting porches and canopied entrance.

The reference in the chamber of commerce brochure to the city's hotels being "put to the test" referred principally to an expansion of the Hotel Roanoke in 1891, which added a number of bedrooms and remodeled extensively the part of the hotel that faced west. The timber-stucco motif was continued and a large wraparound porch built to face both west and south. The work, from an accounting point of view, increased the book value of the property from $45,000 to $125,000, certainly a significant investment for the time.

ABOVE Greyhound bus at the Hotel's entrance. The railroad's General Office Building and automobiles date this photograph to the early or mid-'30s. *Courtesy of the Historical Society of Western Virginia.*

Hotel Roanoke faced a much sterner test in 1898, when, around 1:30 p.m. on the afternoon of July 1, a fire broke out in the kitchen and quickly spread through the frame structure. A photograph taken from across the railroad tracks shows smoke pouring from a half dozen orifices and the lawn filled with spectators and littered with materials salvaged—or at least thrown—from the burning building. The *Roanoke Times* recalled the event in its fiftieth anniversary edition of November 30, 1936:

> *As the blaze soared and it was evident that the fire department was unable to control it, hundreds of men rushed in from the Roanoke Machine Works and assisted in saving much of the furniture and carpets and destroying thousands of dollars worth of hotel equipment in their efforts to save something from the flames. Beds, dressers, mattresses and other furniture, including bowls and pitchers with which many of the rooms were equipped, were hurled from the second and third floor windows, while carpets were wrenched from the floors and piled out in the greatest confusion. Willing hands on the outside were ready to drag the furnishings to vantage points on the lawn to the south and west of the blazing building, all of which was practically destroyed with the exception of the east wing. The roof of the west wing was burned and the interior was gutted. The lobby and office were disfigured by flames, but the construction held intact.*

There is no record of injuries, even in the face of the putative helpers' misplaced zeal.

For a time, it was feared that the entire hotel would have to be rebuilt, but this turned out to be a too-pessimistic view. It was shut down for several months while repair work continued, and by the end of September, a limited number of guests began returning. In October, a double wedding was held to signal, in effect, that the Hotel was again open for business.

For a few weeks, such guests as were registered took their meals in the railroad depot dining room. Although not affiliated in any way with the Hotel, its cuisine was of a quality to give the place a reputation for good dining. Carter Burgess, a prominent Roanoker, was an aide to General Dwight D. Eisenhower in the Second World War and subsequently a notable figure in American industry—and, incidentally, son-in-law of the late R.H. Smith, former president of the Norfolk and Western Railway. He remembered being taken to dinner there by his father, an employee of the Railway

OPPOSITE, TOP The 1898 fire attracted hundreds of sightseers and shut down the Hotel for several months. *Courtesy of Special Collections, University Libraries, Virginia Tech.*

OPPOSITE, BOTTOM The Virginia Association of Local Fire Insurance Agents met in the Hotel in 1920. *Courtesy of the Historical Society of Western Virginia.*

22ᵗʰ Annual Convention of
Va. Association of Local Fire Ins. Agts.
Roanoke, Va. Sept. 22-23, 1920

Express Company. It was, he said, his father's "idea of a treat" during the Depression. He recalled that during this time, Railway Express was one of the offices that moved into the Hotel because of an inability to pay its own rent in those difficult days.

Although the railroad was forced to shut down the Hotel temporarily and take the loss of revenue, there was never a thought of closing it. After only sixteen years, Hotel Roanoke was already firmly situated as a Roanoke institution with a ripening if not exactly mature tradition, and the railroad owners were determined to hold the course.

So the hotel that sprang from the blackened ruins was rebuilt…and rebuilt…and rebuilt in one form or another over the next sixty years or so. What with new wings, alterations and additions, there was left at the end only a globe chandelier said to have been in the original building for posterity to touch or even see. In 1916, the old East Wing was torn down and replaced with a new three-story, seventy-two-room addition. Most of the bedrooms were equipped with private baths, and a number of private dining rooms were installed as well.

By 1931, even this relatively new addition was out of date with the increasing spate of automobile travel. The railroad was willing to spend substantially—$225,000—in this Depression year to make its showpiece more attractive. (Norfolk and Western was in a bullish mood, for simultaneously it was putting up a new eight-story office building across the street from the Hotel, immediately north of the 1896 offices.) For that money, it added to the Hotel forty thousand square feet of floor space, 75 rooms (for a total of 250 in the entire Hotel) and a sixty-car garage. The garage was not the only gesture to advancing technology. Rooms were equipped with electric fans; movable telephones that could be plugged in at four different locations; large closets that lighted automatically when the door was opened; a combination shower and tub bath; and running ice water. All this, reported the *Norfolk and Western Magazine*, put Hotel Roanoke "in a position to enter its 50th year and all the years to come with adequate accommodations and increased comforts for a patronage which has grown steadily since its rambling old ancestor looked down upon the vigorous beginnings of a new city in 1882."

Increased comfort, certainly, for that was the always-moving goal of the Hotel; but "adequate accommodations" widely missed the mark. Only seven years later came the major rebuilding program, budgeted at $1,050,000, exclusive of furnishings. The $225,000 spent for the 1931 work, on the other hand, included furnishings. What

OPPOSITE   Main entrance to Hotel Roanoke, November 1931. *Courtesy of N&W Photo, K.L. Miller Collection.*

came out of the 1937–38 work was symbolized by the grand Tudor entrance, at once imposing and embracing. It was this image of Hotel Roanoke that was photographed, sketched or carried away in the memories of all who passed through the doors.

Still, what was taken away had a memorable charm of its own. The old deep porches, shaded by vines, were charming gathering spots for guests—and others. Elizabeth Bowles, later a Roanoke City councilwoman and one of the principal missionaries in the successful effort to bring the Miss Virginia Pageant to the Hotel, said that in her

ABOVE Rooms 128 and 129—reserved for Hollins College women. *Courtesy of N&W Photo, K.L. Miller Collection.*

OPPOSITE, TOP Hotel Roanoke in the early 1920s. *Courtesy of N&W Photo, K.L. Miller Collection.*

OPPOSITE, BOTTOM Flower bed and driveway, date unknown. *Courtesy of N&W Photo, K.L. Miller Collection.*

teens she would persuade her father to take her the Hotel so she could sit in a porch rocker. Bill Gearhart on Saturday afternoons would climb over the railings and chat with a railroad official who lived in the Hotel. "He was always good for a quarter, so I could go to the movies," Gearhart told an interviewer. Fred Walker, who came to the Hotel as director of sales in 1962, had "heard stories of how certain representatives of the world's oldest profession would come over to the Hotel and sit on the porch, sip lemonade and, for all I know, complete various business arrangements." Years later, Walker was visited in his office by a woman who, though attractive, was to a critical eye perhaps a trifle past the blush of youth. She said that she and two of her ladies were on their way to Florida, and she wondered if perhaps the Hotel would be interested in…well, you know. Courteously and firmly, Walker declined to discuss any such proposal. No, he said, the Hotel was not and never was interested in…well, you know. The woman took the rebuff in good spirit, saying, "Well, no harm trying," and departed the premises.

George B. Post and Sons, a New York architectural firm whose specialty was hotel design, rebuilt the entire West Wing. Sweeping away the old porches, the architects moved the main entrance a few degrees from south to southwest, added 181 guest rooms on five floors and a penthouse and used 524,000 bricks, one thousand tons of structural steel and 5,500 cubic yards of concrete in the process. It was also the first hotel in the country to be engineered for air conditioning. The job included a new one-hundred-car garage, a large number of parking spaces and tasteful landscaping. Inside, the designers created a new lobby and reception area, dining room, Pine Room, Writing Room, Palm Court and ballroom.

Outside, there was to be "a veritable oasis amidst business and industry," as announced by its creator, A.A. Farnham, the Harvard-trained professor of landscape architecture at Virginia Polytechnic Institute. Its principal feature was a large—145 feet by 120 feet—formal garden behind the dining room, planted with six thousand tulip bulbs and quantities of perennials and roses, with mimosa trees shading the walkways through the garden. The gardens were shielded from the sight and sound of bordering city streets by hedges and trees. It was planned as a quiet spot "for teas, meetings of garden clubs and for possible use by convention groups." In later years, a high-ranking officer of the railroad, viewing the garden from his office window across the street, would sometimes call the manager to report that unauthorized persons were in the garden picking flowers and ought to be stopped immediately. The landscaping also included the installation of a reflecting pool in front of the entrance. It was 35 feet in diameter, set in the middle of a 78-foot circle planted in grass, shrubs and flowers. Around this reflecting pool in later years, Miss Virginia candidates ritually gathered for their traditional swimsuit photograph, blossoms that, like the tulips in the garden, regularly caught the eye of railroad employees clustered in four or five stories of windows in the General Office Buildings.

The lobby, paneled in American black walnut an inch and a half thick, was furnished for appearance and comfort. Among the conventional pieces were black marble tables 150 years old, three rosewood chairs, applewood tables, a Chinese credenza and three chandeliers, all at least a century old. Large portraits of George Washington and Robert E. Lee, acquired in 1894, were hung on the walls.

The registration desk laced the front door. Above it was a series of murals tracing the history of the New World—the *Mayflower*, Pilgrims and Indians, John Smith and Pocahontas marrying, Patrick Henry orating and an old South plantation. Hung from the ceiling nearby was the 1882 globe chandelier, emblazoned with a pineapple design, the symbol of hospitality.

The Hotel's entrance before the 1938 rebuilding lay in the area around the Oval Room, then called the Palm Court, and the Pine Room, and so if there was an "original" part of the building, it was here. The Palm Court was so called because of the dozen potted palms placed on its perimeter. It was adjacent to a glassed-in porch from which guests, lounging in the wicker chairs fashionable at the time, could enjoy the view of a large garden. In the 1937 remodeling, the glassed-in porch became Peacock Alley and the garden site became the Crystal Ballroom. The Palm Court, for its part, was given perhaps the most ingenious and possibly most elaborate treatment in the entire remodeling. Eighteen coats of paint were applied to the ceiling to achieve the desired deep blue night sky effect, and on it was painted the configuration of celestial bodies as they appeared in the heavens on November 1, 1852, the day the first train arrived in Big Lick. A green carpet, said to have been the "largest of its kind ever made," measured fifty-four by forty-one feet. A large light hung from the middle of the ceiling over a massive, specially made table in the center of the room.

The Pine Room was paneled in warm knotty pine and hung about with traditional prints and a painting of the Roanoke Valley by a now unknown artist of the time. Two antique Windsor chairs, put together with pegs, sat for many years on either side of the black Italian marble fireplace, which, like the others in the Hotel, was decorative, not functional.

The Crystal Ballroom, which would become the heart of the Hotel's business and social life, measured 46 by 118 feet and was done in green, gold and red. Three crystal chandeliers, made in Czechoslovakia and originally fitted for gas lighting, were suspended from an arched ceiling, under which, as the years rolled by, people danced, cattle lowed, diners dined, politicians denounced and beauty contestants preened.

The dining room, which later earned the Mobil Four-Star award for dining excellence for eight consecutive years, like the lobby and Oval and Pine Rooms, was

located just about where it was originally, but with a new curved bay facing north and overlooking Farnham's tulip garden. It was "oyster-white in color and Georgian in design," according to a contemporary account. Dogwood, the Virginia state blossom, was used as the decorative motif and repeated in the design for the new china. The same account reported that the china was brought to Roanoke by rail, 1,663 dozen pieces, plus four tons of silverware.

Supporting the dining room was a new, large and state-of-the-art kitchen, including an ice machine capable of producing more than two tons of ice each day. (By coincidence, two tons was also the capacity of the new laundry.)

Upstairs, the new guest rooms—making a total of 310 in the entire Hotel—featured the new air conditioning, new furniture, indirect lighting, radio, tiled tub and shower, safety locks, "wine-colored carpets of distinctive design" and, as a final inducement, Venetian blinds plus circulating ice water. There was a penthouse, too, on the seventh floor, overlooking the city through huge gabled windows in a story-and-a-half living room. The penthouse's first tenant was H.W. Shields, vice president and general manager of Pocahontas Coal & Coke Company, who lived there with his family for many years.

That family included Roanoker Harry Hewitt, then fifteen; his mother; his aunt; and Shields, his grandfather. Hewitt lived in the penthouse apartment off and on for the next twenty-five years or so, during summer vacations from boarding school and college, on leave from the army and while working at the railroad's Roanoke Terminal. The apartment was also the first home for him and his wife, Joyce, for a few months in the early 1950s. (One memory from those days involves a mouse watching Joyce write thank-you notes.)

Both W.J. Jenks, the railroad's president, and E.R. Johnson, a director and a man of substance in the community, wanted the penthouse apartment as his own. Shields, executive in charge of a major NW subsidiary (later the Pocahontas Land Company), pointed out that the two men's wives were both interested in gardening and that the penthouse, for all its cachet and other advantages, had no garden. Shields, on the other hand, cared nothing for gardening, and thus almost by default did he get the key to 701.

In the penthouse, the Shields family enjoyed the same level of service as other guests. Beds were made up and fresh towels and soap were provided daily, rooms were cleaned, waste baskets were emptied and room service was only a telephone call away. Outside telephone calls cost fifteen cents (which added up to a sizable

OPPOSITE   The Pine Room, *top*, and the registration desk, circa 1947. *Top: Courtesy of the Historical Society of Western Virginia; bottom: Courtesy of Special Collections, University Libraries, Virginia Tech.*

Above: The Fountain Room of happy memory. *Courtesy of the Historical Society of Western Virginia*; *opposite, top*: beauty salon customers, both from 1947. *Courtesy of the Historical Society of Western Virginia*; *opposite, bottom*: a typical guest room in the 1931 wing. *Courtesy of N&W Photo, K.L. Miller Collection.*

BEAUTY SALON

sum, Hewitt recalls, in his dating days). And like all the other guest rooms, the penthouse apartment had a daily rental rate: the two bedrooms, two baths, dining room, "marvelous kitchen" and living room cost nine dollars a day. There was also a terrace, but ambient dust and locomotive soot made it unusable. However, some other guests in the Hotel found a way to reach the terrace for their own intimate purposes and did so, even looking into the apartment's windows until "Mother, unhappy with these goings-on, persuaded Mr. Hyde to put a special lock on the terrace door."

Meals were not included. Shields had his breakfast—and frequently lunch—at a downtown cafeteria, sometimes accompanied by young Harry. Dinner, on the other hand, was always in the Regency Room. Jenks had decreed that there would be no reservations, so seating was first-come, first-served. Hewitt recalls many trips from the seventh floor to the dining room to see if there was a line of waiting diners. "Reservations or not, we somehow always had the same table," he says.

Coming in from his day's work as a railroad yard clerk, Hewitt would "clomp across the lobby in my work clothes and boots and carrying my lunch bucket to the desk to pick up my mail." Once, in the moving-out process, Joyce, thanks to a balky elevator, found herself crossing the lobby with a dishpan full of cleaning materials for their new home, two unusual counterpoints to the Hotel's elegance.

All that was in the future when the Hotel's new look was officially unveiled to the world on September 15, 1938, just about a year from the day the Norfolk and Western

OPPOSITE   The Tulip Garden, 1948. *Courtesy of N&W Photo, K.L. Miller Collection.*

ABOVE   Employee cafeteria in the kitchen. *Courtesy of the Historical Society of Western Virginia.*

Photographs of the parts of the hotel seldom seen by guests. *This page, top*: inside the cashier's office. *Courtesy of N&W Photo, K.L. Miller Collection; this page, bottom*: the laundry. *Courtesy of Special Collections, University Libraries, Virginia Tech; opposite, top*: employees working in the valet shop. *Courtesy of N&W Photo, K.L. Miller Collection; opposite, bottom*: kitchen staff at work. *Courtesy of Special Collections, University Libraries, Virginia Tech.*

announced the project. The *Roanoke Times* of the day before, from which much in this account has been taken, published a series of congratulatory advertisements from the Hotel's contractors and other well-wishers. Among them were comradely greetings from the Patrick Henry and Ponce de Leon Hotels. Kimbalton Lime Company of Shawsville praised the hotel and its building contractor, J.A. Jones Construction Company, for "A 'Beautiful' Hotel and a 'Beautiful' Piece of Brickwork." Smithfield Packing Co., Inc., mentioned that the Hotel would be using its products in the dining room. Mick or Mack, "Roanoke-owned Grocers," declared, "It is our sincere pleasure, and unsolicited, to extend congratulatory greetings." And so on, from the Murphy Door Bed Company through Densmore Poultry Farms to a dozen more, eager to pay for the privilege of associating themselves in public with the splendid new-old Hotel on the Hill.

A half-page ad was from the Hotel itself, announcing open house hours (10:00 a.m. to 5:00 p.m.) for the next day, and listing prices for its meals in its "stately Main Dining Room." Breakfast ranged from $0.35 to $0.75, luncheon from $0.60 to $0.90 and dinner from $1.10 to $1.50. Respective menus were not shown. Rates for the rooms in the new wing began at $3.00 and in the East Wing at $2.50. The ad was signed by

ABOVE The parking garage, 1951. *Courtesy of N&W Photo, K.L. Miller Collection.*

Kenneth R. Hyde, general manager, and George. L. Denison, resident manager, a pair to figure largely, even seminally, in the Hotel's subsequent history.

The opening celebrations were actually spread over two "Nights." The first, on September 15, was "Roanoke Night," when the parquetry floor of the Crystal Ballroom first felt the slide and shuffle of dancing feet. Don Bestor's Orchestra played, the same Don Bestor whose band was once part of Jack Benny's radio show. Tickets were limited to five hundred couples and cost three dollars each. As a notable, not to say extraordinary, community event, Roanoke Night ranked with the "initiatory German" of more than a half century before and was to be equaled and possibly surpassed only by Governors' Night in 1967 and the Closing Banquet in 1989.

"Well, it was a grand party," wrote "Candida" (nom de plume of Dorothy Hancock, *Roanoke Times* reporter) in the next morning's newspaper, in an account curiously echoing the reporting of the first German in 1883:

> *The town will be talking for years to come about the night its Hotel Roanoke opened, and everybody who could get a reservation hauled out his tux or tails, or bought a new dress, as the case may be, and went to the ball. Went to dine, first, perhaps, in the magnificent rose and white dining room and then to dance to Don Bestor's music in the ballroom, and to wander between dances through Peacock Alley, in the blue light of the Palm Court, and down into the great lobby. It was a little hard to remember at times that we were really still in Roanoke—even the familiar faces on every side might have belonged to shipmates on some super luxury liner.*
>
> *While giving our fancy sandals a rest, we had a fine time looking over all the new evening gowns parading past us. The girls looked mighty fine, there's no doubt about it. All the cerise and violet tones reported from the Paris openings were there, and the velvets, heavy satins and brocades the couturiers have gone mad about. We saw several hoopskirts, ranging from Tee Gregory's red plaid, which she seemed to have no trouble managing in dancing, to a black taffeta version of the Jezebel-inspired mode. Mary Wise Parrott's aqua velvet was a beauty, as was Tay Parrot's gold lame with a little bustle flounce to it. Mary Stone Moore (Miss) was lovely in a dress of white net with little pineapple slices of gathered net for trimming. Carol Clark's dress of flowing net in violet and purple was nothing short of an achievement.*
>
> *Hair was up and hair was down—some intended as the former was nearer the latter before the evening waned. The main impression we gathered was that the off-the-neck style hasn't as yet been unreservedly adopted by our sister townswomen.*
>
> *The gentlemen looked pretty handsome too. Even the one asleep out on the porch when the dance broke up looked rather distinguished in his slumbers.*
>
> *It was a grand party. More we cannot say.*

Razing of the right wing, March 1931.
Courtesy of N&W Photo, K.L. Miller Collection.

For John Eure, then a *Roanoke Times* reporter and later an editor, it was grand party too. He took his date home from the ball and got engaged. "The atmosphere certainly helped."

The second opening event was called "Hotel Men's Night" and attracted professional hoteliers from all over the state for dinner. The headliners were Governors James H. Price of Virginia and Homer A. Holt of West Virginia. W.J. Jenks, president of Norfolk and Western Railway, was there, and so was E.R. Johnson, a NW director and former president of Rotary International. The railroad was further represented by Vice President Sydney F. Small and almost certainly a cadre of lesser officials, unnamed in the press. Junius P. Fishburn, publisher of the *Roanoke Times* and its afternoon sister, the *World-News*, and a major figure in the city's business life, was the toastmaster. Reverend Dr. R.A. Lapsley Jr., pastor of Roanoke's First Presbyterian Church, delivered the invocation. By any standard, it was a gathering of the mighty, for neither the first nor the last time in the Hotel's history.

Chapter 2

NOT ALL BRICK, BUT PEOPLE TOO

With the unveiling of the new West Wing, Hotel Roanoke could be said to have entered its modern stage. The physical plant was superb, its location ideal, its reputation immaculate and growing. Overseeing and managing this glittering and promising property were two men who would lead it into a new and golden age covering a quarter of a century: Sydney Small and Kenneth Hyde. Small, who had begun work for the railroad in 1911 as a forty-dollars-a-month clerk, had been named vice president/assistant to the president in 1935. His portfolio was principally public relations and legislative matters, and over the years, he had managed them both so successfully that the railroad won several awards for public relations achievements, especially in advertising. In politics, he was such a familiar figure in Virginia legislative circles, deftly and skillfully wielding influence—if not downright power—on behalf of the railroad and its many causes, that in time he became known as the "forty-first senator." His Cadillac's license tag number was an impressive 25. Small also served as Roanoke's mayor, and it was largely through his pervasive and persuasive presence in local politics that the interests of the city and those of the railroad were widely thought to be virtually congruent and possibly identical. "When the railroad sneezes, Roanoke reaches for a handkerchief," a community saying for many years, was not altogether inaccurate, given the large number of railroad employees there.

Small recognized clearly that in Hotel Roanoke he had at hand not only a gleaming prize that reflected the railroad itself but also a powerful hospitality-dispensing machine to which he had the key. When the railroad's inner circle discussed the Hotel and the talk turned to its financial support, his was undoubtedly the firmest voice in its favor, especially when it involved the million-dollar expansion in 1938 (and more to come in the years ahead).

Across the street from Small's office and easily visible from there was the imposing new façade housing Hyde and Denison, general manager and resident manager, respectively. They constituted a team that until Hyde's death in 1963 relentlessly maintained and even enhanced Hotel Roanoke's standards of quality performance. Hyde had returned as general manager in 1938 as the new wing was being completed after an absence of three years. He had first come to the Hotel in 1928 as assistant manager; though he was only twenty-one, he had already accumulated experience in the hospitality trade at a hotel in Winchester, Virginia. He was named manager in 1929 and resigned in 1935 to become manager of Richmond's John Marshall Hotel.

George Denison. *Courtesy of Special Collections, University Libraries, Virginia Tech.*

Hyde, darkly handsome, dedicated and charming, devoted much of his time to promotional matters and soliciting convention business for the new hotel. In an editorial tribute at the time of his death, the *Roanoke World-News* said, "More than any other man, Ken Hyde made a science of obtaining conventions for the Star City....He played a tremendous part in keeping the city prosperous....Ken Hyde indeed filled the picture of the professional innkeeper... courtly, affable, polite, friendly in speech and attractive in manner. He was a credit to Roanoke and his passing is a sad loss to the community." It was a fine epitaph for the Hotel's manager.

He was also, according to Janet Jenkins, a religious man who lived his faith at work. He was "a fine gentleman, a devoted family man...who was concerned over the welfare of all Hotel Roanoke employees." He "enjoyed the respect and affection of all the hotel's managers and employees. I never heard a criticism of him." "A grand man" is the way Fred Walker, another Hyde subordinate and later a successor as the Hotel's general manager, described him.

Mrs. Jenkins went to work for the Hotel as a part-time secretary in 1950 and retired from it thirty years later as general manager, so she worked for Hyde for thirteen years. "He was a strong taskmaster, but a kindly one—and so enthralled with the hotel business that he was sometimes oblivious to his surroundings." One day, early in her career, the secretarial staff decided to put this apparent detachment to a test.

> *It was around Halloween, and I had a Groucho Marx pair of glasses with mustache to take home. I bet the girls I could wear them into his office* [for dictation] *and he would never notice them. Well, it was a good fifteen to twenty minutes before he even looked at me. I could hear girlish giggles outside the door. When he did look, he was highly incensed and gave me a lecture on appropriate Hotel Roanoke behavior in the office.*
>
> *Also, I was a great soft whistler. One day, he came into my cubicle and quoted "whistling girls and cackling hens will never come to any good end." I apologized and desisted. Several weeks later, he came into the cubicle again and said, "JJ, I miss your whistling." So I laughed and resumed—and haven't stopped to this day.*

Roaming the Hotel every day was a part of the gregarious Hyde's job, especially enjoyable because it provided the opportunity to talk to the staff at all levels. Occasionally, these tours bore fruit—literally. One former employee recalled that Hyde would sometimes stop in the kitchen, pick up a banana and eat it. "Charge it to Mr. Griffith," he would say with a smile and continue his rounds. (Griffith was the executive steward at the time.)

The outside view of the Hotel's general manager was essentially the same as the inside. As a journalist, John Eure had a continuing view of the man at work. "I saw Ken Hyde three or four times a week as a matter of course. He was accommodating and amiable, as he should have been to reporters; he had a good sense of public relations and what reporters wanted; but he was also a fine man."

Such was the man who assumed command of the "new" Hotel Roanoke. On hand when he returned to take up his new post was George Denison, a veteran of the hotel business. He had worked for a Florida hotel in 1925, briefly for Hotel Roanoke in 1927 and then with a New York hotel and at the Hotel Chamberlin in Hampton, Virginia, before returning to Hotel Roanoke in 1930, there to stay until his retirement as manager in 1964. During Hyde's three-year absence (1935–38), Denison served as manager. (When World War II came, history repeated itself: Hyde left for service with the navy, and Denison became manager. Upon Hyde's return after the war, they were designated co-managers.)

From 1938 on, at least in the last two or three years of peace before the world was irrevocably changed, Hotel Roanoke sailed on its serene way, polishing its success as assiduously as it did the handsome paneling in the lobby. About the Hotel's staff,

MRS. JENKINS
Convention Sec'y

Fred Walker, general manager in the late 1960s, observed that they were "the salt of the earth. If the words 'loyal' and 'dedicated' can be used anywhere, they should describe these people. They all of them—dining room waiters, bellmen, room service waiters, maids, desk clerks, secretaries, dishwashers, cooks, sales people, most of them anonymous—did their jobs day by day, and did them well."

There were others too, less anonymous, who became part of the Hotel's legend, in one case through fame, in another through sheer longevity—and quality. In June 1942, J. Ed (Deacon) Brown, assistant headwaiter, completed an astonishing sixty years of service with the Hotel and was honored by having his photograph on the front of the dining room menu.

Hotel Roanoke

Congratulates

J. Ed. Brown

JUNE

1882 1945

63 Years' Service

1882

1945

OPPOSITE   Janet Jenkins, *left*, the "great lady" of the Hotel for many years, discusses convention bookings with Walter Chapman, catering manager, and Judy Walker, secretary. *Courtesy of the Historical Society of Western Virginia.*

ABOVE   *Courtesy of Norfolk Southern Corporation.*

Courtesy of Virginia Room, Roanoke Public Libraries.

Incredibly, he was still autographing them for patrons in early 1945. "He made quite a good thing out of signing those menus," recalled one who observed Brown in action, "because each autograph was usually good for a couple of dollars." (Food costs shown in that wartime menu reflected government-imposed price controls but, even so, were remarkable: Two lamb chops, $0.95. Peach Melba, $0.30. The most expensive item was a planked steak for two, at $4.00.)

In honoring Deacon Brown's anniversary, the old gentleman—who might well have brought dinner to Frederick Kimball—was given two fifty-dollar Defense Bonds by Hyde and Denison in a ballroom ceremony crowded with Brown's fellow employees. "I worked in the original wooden building when all we had was 38 rooms, with iron beds, hard chairs and bad lights. Now look at this place," he said. "It's the finest in the country." In his six-decade-plus career, Brown served such luminaries as Charles Evans Hughes, William Jennings Bryan, J.P. Morgan (reportedly fond of the Hotel's scrambled eggs) and Mrs. Calvin Coolidge and put his four children through college.

Not far behind was William Campbell, who in 1948 celebrated his forty-fifth anniversary and for whom "a lifetime as a waiter" was synonymous with "a lifetime of happiness." When he started out in 1903, "the place was almost a log cabin. There was a porch all the way around the building and the only way you could get to the rooms was from that porch. Many is the time I've taken those steps two at a time to keep warm in winter." Like Deacon Brown, Campbell sent all his children—four sons and two daughters—to college, and like him too, he had his photograph on the front of a congratulatory menu.

To say that fame came to Fred Brown is less accurate than to say that fame came to Fred Brown's creation. For it was in 1940—when Deacon Brown had been a waiter for only fifty-two years, and two years after the Tudor entrance was installed—that Chef Brown invented Hotel Roanoke's signature peanut soup. Manager Hyde had been after Chef Brown to produce something new and different for the Hotel. Chef "kept on putting things together" until, after a long period of experimentation, during which he established ordinary peanut butter as the prime ingredient, he declared himself satisfied. Favorable reaction was immediate, as was the new soup's fame. Requests for the recipe came from all over the world, and for a time, Fred Walker recalls that the Hotel closely guarded the recipe and declined to share it. In the face of hundreds of requests every year, "we finally printed it and sent it to anyone who asked. They had probably been our guests, after all." It has since been reprinted by the Hotel in its own promotional material and in many published cookbooks; patient readers of this book will find it here as well.

Brown started with the Hotel on July 4, 1922, while he was still in high school. He was a "runner," fetching supplies from the storeroom to the kitchen, and after graduating from high school, he worked his way up on the food preparation side: "boiler cook, fry cook, then roast cook, then assistant chef—grand marche—that's the cold meat cook," he told Ann Fox Sprague, a writer for the *Norfolk and Western Magazine*, at the time of his retirement in May 1964. In 1927, he left the Hotel to improve his trade elsewhere as assistant chef or chef. But like so many others, including Denison, Hyde and Warren Webb, he found the lure of the old place irresistible. So after grazing in other pastures, notably the Greenbrier Hotel, he returned to his beloved Hotel Roanoke as executive chef in 1937. Good humored, he was, and a perfectionist, but not temperamental—except once, according to Warren Webb, who was steward at the time. In a moment of uncharacteristic irascibility following a dispute with another employee, Brown ran him out of his kitchen with such energy that he lost his false teeth.

Sprague recalled being invited to lunch with Chef at his own table in the kitchen, a rare privilege for an outsider. From that table after planning discussions with Lee Griffith, the Hotel's executive steward (and predecessor of Warren Webb), came the dishes and specialties that delighted diners for many years. The continuing cuisine was not limited to "Southern"—peanut soup, of course, and country ham, fried chicken, chess pie and all the traditional accustomed Dixie trappings. The menu listed seafoods (especially from Virginia), lamb, beef, salads and all the other items that kept diners returning time and again for memorable dining.

Griffith's Hotel Roanoke career began in 1930, and when he retired in May 1969—coincidentally the same day as Chef Brown—he was executive steward. He was responsible for buying all the food and beverages served from the kitchen and helping prepare the menus and even had a hand in the design of the new kitchen for the 1938 remodeling.

Chef Brown, being the chef, was always the star of Hotel Roanoke cuisine and king of the kitchen but never more so than at Thanksgiving. It was perhaps the busiest day in the Hotel's year, at least during the 1950s and '60s. For that day, all the furniture was removed from the lobby both to protect it from and make room for the crowds attending the annual Virginia Military Institute–Virginia Polytechnic Institute football game in Roanoke. VPI's headquarters were in the Hotel, VMI's in the Hotel Patrick Henry. Nobody got the day off. Hundreds of box lunches were put up in the big kitchen for the game attendees. One Thanksgiving, 1,200 persons were served dinner, at the rate of three thirty-pound turkeys for every 100 diners. The cranberry sauce was prepared personally by Joe Brown, the assistant chef who in time succeeded Fred

OPPOSITE, TOP   The Regency Room in the late 1940s. *Courtesy of N&W Photo, K.L. Miller Collection.*

OPPOSITE, BOTTOM   The Green Room, May 1932. *Courtesy of N&W Photo, K.L. Miller Collection.*

Brown. Joe Brown (no relation to Fred) served in the navy during the Second World War, working in his ship's galley and serving in a gun crew as well.

If Chef Brown was the undisputed king behind the swinging doors, the Regency Room itself had its own monarch—in fact, two. These were Charles Hofer, maître d'hôtel, and his assistant, Joseph Brenneis, whose European training added a cosmopolitan counterpoint to the warm southerness of Hotel Roanoke. Hofer's unflappability was sorely tested in the Regency Room one night. He was escorting a Roanoke matron of some standing to her dinner table when her stride faltered perceptibly. Turning, Hofer observed what the woman already knew: that her panties had fallen to her ankles. The two carried off the incident with great savoir faire, the woman carefully stepping out of the garment, Hofer coolly pocketing it and both continuing on to the table. After dinner, the woman retrieved it from Hofer, who had carefully put it away in his desk. "A classic example of style," was the way the incident was described by the manager who later recounted the anecdote.

Hofer and Brenneis were natives of Vienna and served their apprenticeship in that city's Hotel Metropole. Friends, they worked separately in Paris, London, Geneva and the Riviera and were reunited in Holland. The pair moved to the United States in 1927 and worked in several U.S. cities. Hofer came to the Hotel Roanoke in 1932, Brenneis in 1938. Duties consisted of arranging for all of the banquet activities in the Hotel, not just the routine meals of the area's various service clubs that regularly met there, but also the large-scale meals—breakfasts, luncheons and dinners—associated with the conventions.

In their time and later, when 150 conventions each year were commonplace, much of the banquet activity was in the Crystal Ballroom. It could accommodate over one thousand at a meeting, nine hundred for meals and six hundred for dinner dances. Sometimes, all three events were held consecutively on the same day. Billy Davis and Alphonso "Alex" Alexander, banquet managers after Hofer and Brenneis's time, still boast of the efficient turnaround they achieved with their staff when a black-tie cattle auction in the Crystal Ballroom in the 1960s was followed by a Roanoke Symphony Ball that same night. A VPI student told a reporter afterward that "it was purely different, leading a Hereford on sawdust under chandeliers." The sawdust was spread over rubber mats to protect the floor during the auction. Billy Davis recalled later that the lingering aroma after the auction was noticeable, but with the aid of "maybe hundreds of spray cans of deodorizers, we cleared it out quickly" to set up the room for the ball a few hours later.

Billy Davis and Alex Alexander were for many years so omnipresent at the Hotel's social events that they became virtually interchangeable parts of the mechanism. Davis started working in the dining room while he was still a high school student in 1943; Alexander began as a hall boy in 1947. They both retired when the Hotel closed in 1989, Davis as banquet manager, Alexander as his assistant. They were trained in hotel service, as they

Warren Webb, food and beverage manager, became busier than ever when Virginia amended its liquor laws. *Courtesy of the Historical Society of Western Virginia.*

trained others, in a "hand-me-down" fashion—which is not to be taken to mean shabby or worn-out. It meant teaching new employees the style and quality that was part of the Hotel way of doing business. "Old-timers taught us that quality begins at the front door," said Davis. "We taught the same lesson to new ones." Their work hours stretched endlessly across the clock, often from early in the morning to well after midnight, because "if there was an event going on, one of us was always there," Alexander said. These two men, dignified, able, courteous, epitomized the character of Hotel Roanoke to the very end. They not only passed on the tradition—they were part of it.

The heart of the Hotel's food and banquet service began, of course, in the huge kitchen. Typically, the Hotel's cooks arrived for work at 5:30 a.m. to prepare for the day. Cooks and waiters had their own jargon: scrambled eggs with visible white were "showing a little country"; eggs that were too runny required "tightening up." French toast was cut thick from an unsliced loaf. "Last night's un-ordered baked potatoes were this morning's hash-browns," according to Webb. A farmer from Franklin County would come in every day to pick up food scraps for his pigs, and every day he would faithfully return any silverware that had been inadvertently tossed out. After a while, this practice, useful though it was to man and beast alike, was stopped by health authorities.

The Saturday Night Buffet, in its time as compelling a tradition as the Sunday Brunch, was in later years a triumph of southern cuisine. There was shrimp, steamboat round, ham, turkey and fried chicken as the principal dishes, plus of course the usual vegetables and desserts. All this was priced at $3.50, and in addition, there was dancing on a rather small floor in the middle of the Regency Room. Years earlier, Warren Webb, job-seeking at the Hotel, was told to come back when he turned sixteen (in February 1944). This he did, deciding to stop at the Hotel that very day, a Saturday. He was hired on the spot by James Hunter, the assistant manager. "Start right away," he told young Webb, who protested that he was on his way to a movie. "You want a job or you want to go to a movie?" asked Hunter. Given such a stark choice, Webb picked the job. It paid him $100 a month and one meal a day. The Hotel at this time was housing army air force and later navy flying officers taking four weeks of wartime class work and flight instructions in DC3s at Roanoke's Woodrum Field. They and those with wives were housed in the south wing and, having turned over their food ration books—everybody had one during the war—to the Hotel, were fed in the Regency Room as residents. For their relaxation, the government took over the Pine Room to serve as an officers' club. It was fitted out with a jukebox playing what are today's golden oldies, a small dance floor, a bar and even a guard—usually the officer of the day—at the door. It was there that Warren Webb went to work, serving as bartender, setting up soft drinks and generally keeping the place clean. He worked at the Hotel for a while and left and then, as so many others did, finally came back to stay. He

retired in 1985 after twenty-five years as purchasing and stores manager, responsible for the workings of the kitchen and storeroom.

In its own way, the officers' club contributed to Roanoke's social life. The same Helen Fitzpatrick who recalled her parents dressing in costume for the German Club likewise remembered USO dances at the Hotel for its resident flyers, the navy men "so handsome in their dress whites." Bachelor officers would find dates at Hollins College or elsewhere in the area, much as the German Club members did in the early days. One officer was married to Gail Patrick, a popular movie star of the time, who later had a kick-off role in the city's United Fund campaign one year. She was "a lovely person, and much in demand at community functions."

Another "name" visitor to the officers' club was Morton Downey, who in 1944 brought his orchestra to the Hotel and broadcast his regular national network radio

ABOVE   The various parlors could accommodate meetings, parties and poker and bridge games or, in this case, dinner. *Courtesy of Special Collections, University Libraries, Virginia Tech.*

The model removes her gloves to switch on a guest room radio in this 1947 photograph. *Courtesy of Special Collections, University Libraries, Virginia Tech.*

program from the Crystal Ballroom. After the show, he had a piano moved into the Pine Room and played for the officers and their guests until nearly two o'clock in the morning.

The war ended; Gail Patrick went back to Hollywood and relative obscurity, the officers and the Pine Room all returned to civilian life and the Hotel began to prepare for business in the postwar world. The smoke of battle had scarcely dissipated when at the end of September 1945, the Norfolk and Western announced another million-dollar facelift at the Hotel, compatible with the Hotel's Tudor style. The project involved mainly the replacement of the four-story wing parallel to the railroad tracks—the south wing—with one of five stories. New bedrooms raised the total to 361, and each room was equipped with on-the-wall radios with a choice of four radio stations. These rooms, incidentally, within sight and sound of railroad operations, exerted an appeal that the architects—Smith, Small and Reeb, of Cleveland—could not have foreseen.

Arthur M. Bixby, a railroad enthusiast and historian, frequently called on the Norfolk and Western on behalf of Dresser Industries, a supplier of railroad equipment. Arriving in Roanoke in the morning from New York via NW No. 1 from Hagerstown, he would find "a Hotel Roanoke porter with a two-wheel cart waiting on the platform beside the sleeper, who would take your luggage and wheel it up the hill to the Hotel. A 25-cent tip was big in those days....Most of the time a desk clerk named Skippy was on duty and assigned me a room on the track side of the Hotel, at my request. While going to sleep, I would listen to the soft chuff-chuffs of the Class Y compound mallets and the sharp barks of the single Class A 2-6-6-4s, identifying them by class from their sound." This ability to distinguish one steam locomotive from another by its sound, while astonishing to some, is not uncommon among knowledgeable rail fans. Dr. Raymond Smoot, later a vice president of Virginia Tech, has recalled that he could do it himself and would occasionally check into the Hotel for the sheer enjoyment it provided him as a guest and rail fan. At least twice in subsequent years, the National Railway Historical Society held its annual meeting there, and the rooms facing the track were the first to be reserved.

On the levels below the new guest rooms, the architects situated a row of small parlors, each handsomely furnished and equipped with a marble—but nonworking—fireplace. These rooms were designed for meetings and small conferences and could easily seat sixteen or eighteen guests for sit-down meals; to accommodate more elaborate events and larger numbers, they could be opened into each other. A small group of senior railroad officers, led by President W.J. Jenks, would from time to time make evening use of three of the parlors: one for cocktails, one for dinner, the third for poker.

The Fountain Room was new—a "modernistic and colorful gathering place" was the way it was described in the *Norfolk and Western Magazine*—with fluted marble

columns supporting the ceiling, a seating capacity of 125 and murals showing Virginia scenes and historical events. Its menu was undemanding and satisfying, and it filled a specific need in the Hotel for an eating place more intimate than the formal Regency Room. Just the same, in those days when "informal" meant something different than it came to mean in later years, most ladies lunching there came in hats and sometimes gloves.

Just as this addition brought the Fountain Room to life, the next major work, in 1955, ended it. The Fountain Room, popular and attractive, had served its purpose

Above: The Hotel around 1950 in an extensively retouched photograph. *Courtesy of N&W Photo, K.L. Miller Collection*; *opposite, top*: a typical '60s family relaxes in their room. *Courtesy of Special Collections, University Libraries, Virginia Tech*; *opposite, bottom*: the living room of the penthouse apartment in 1938. *Courtesy of Special Collections, University Libraries, Virginia Tech.*

and was replaced by a seven-in-the-morning-to-ten-at-night Coffee Shop with a soda bar and seating for an additional one hundred guests. Later, to meet the increasingly diverse tastes of its clientele, the Coffee Shop also disappeared, and the Hotel used the same space for the Windsor Room, the Ad Lib Club (offering food, drink and jazz) and, finally, Jimmy Butler's Comedy Club.

With the 1946–47 work, Hotel Roanoke became completely air-conditioned, a circumstance somewhat at variance with the boast that in the 1938 rebuilding it had become the first hotel to be "scientifically designed for air-conditioning." It seems clear that being designed for cooling and being actually cooled were two different things. In any event, the project also included a major kitchen expansion, adding walk-in refrigerators capable of holding a thousand steaks, and separate kitchen facilities for the Fountain Room. A Turkish bath was also installed. Work started in December 1945 and ended in early 1947, somewhat behind schedule.

Although there would be other guest services instituted—the motel entrance, the swimming pool, a convention exhibition hall, redecorating, attractive watering holes for

Familiar scenes for Hotel-goers: the Writing Room and the Virginia Room, located off the Regency Room, both from 1938, and Peacock Alley in 1943, with its summer wicker furniture. *Opposite, top to bottom: courtesy of Special Collections, University Libraries, Virginia Tech; courtesy of the Historical Society of Western Virginia; above: courtesy of Special Collections, University Libraries, Virginia Tech.*

thirsty conventioneers—there was only one more major construction project to come before the Hotel was closed in 1989. Costing $1.2 million and opening for business in March 1955, a new five-story-and-basement north wing parallel to Jefferson Street added fifty-six guest rooms, the Shenandoah Room for conventions, the Coffee Shop mentioned previously, expanded kitchen space and an employee cafeteria.

Vice President Sydney Small underlined the significance of this "costly addition" when he noted that it was made primarily to accommodate increasing demands for larger convention facilities. The Hotel clearly felt that whereas guests and their families would always be welcome and cosseted with Hotel Roanoke's trademark service and hospitality and would not be ignored, the nation's changing business mores had created a burgeoning convention trade. An investment to meet these increasingly sophisticated and diverse demands would surely bring a return—and, one hoped, a substantial one. The number always to be watched and improved upon was the occupancy rate.

ABOVE Guests at the main entrance in 1949. *Courtesy of Special Collections, University Libraries, Virginia Tech.*

Chapter 3

FILLING THE HOUSE

The convention trade had been part of the Hotel's business from its very beginning. It was not a year old when, in June 1883, the American Institute of Mining Engineers met there. The aim then—to put guests in the rooms and diners at the tables—was the same in 1952. In the new postwar business climate, the Hotel produced and distributed widely a film called *Hospitality Unlimited*. It was directed principally at the convention/business meeting market and showed off the Hotel and its many guest services—although sometimes straining the putative "story line" to do so.

For example, breakfast is brought to one of the film's stars (an opportunity to show off a wheeled cart with a built-in warming unit), and he manages to spill coffee on his shirt through a gap in the front of the handsome dressing gown—far too upscale a garment to be called a bathrobe—he is wearing. The reason he spilled the coffee was that he was using the cup as a baton, keeping time to the music coming from the four-station wall radio he had just turned on. No problem, says the narrator; Hotel Roanoke has a modern laundry to take care of just such mishaps. The laundry is then shown, along with an "ingenious machine" to sew on buttons.

Hospitality Unlimited has at this distance a dated charm: the men all in suits and ties, even when driving along the Parkway in an immense top-down convertible. In the opening scene, Hotel guests arrive on a passenger train hauled by a Norfolk and Western Class J locomotive. The women detrain wearing hats, gloves and furs.

Bellmen escort the guests to their rooms and point out the new amenities: "turn a knob and the weather is at your command" and the "individually wrapped drinking glasses." When the guests order dinner, the film has an opportunity to show the "exclusive dogwood pattern china," kitchen facilities, huge food lockers, the bakeshop and even a machine that manufactures ice "never touched by human hands." After dinner, one of the men offers cigarettes around his table. The waiter offers a light, "a little touch that makes a difference," says the film's narrator.

While the business sessions go on, the women are manicured in the beauty shop, play bridge in the Pine Room and prepare postcards "for the folks back home in the Writing Room." Some of the men, possibly skipping the business session, are in the barbershop or the adjacent health club. One, in shirt and tie, is working out on a stationary bicycle; another, presumably not wearing a shirt and tie, is in the steam bath; and a third is getting a rubdown. The film ends with the executive committee of the organization holding its meeting at the Hotel, approving the motion that "we meet here again next year."

A second film, produced in 1963, shows off new facilities and conveniences installed after *Hospitality Unlimited* was made. There were little things, such as television sets in the rooms and message lights on the telephone; but there were also major additions designed with the business meeting clientele in mind. These included the Shenandoah Room; the Exhibit Hall, fitted out to handle large displays; the Motor Inn for tire conventioneers, overnight guests and townsfolk as well; the new (in 1962) swimming pool; and the noon snacks and evening dancing around it. This film, narrated by the late Robert Porterfield, the man who put Abingdon's Barter Theater on the map, ended with the same happy message as the first film: "My group voted to come back next year."

The year 1963 was when Ken Hyde died and was succeeded as general manager by George Denison. When, slightly more than a year later, Denison himself retired, he turned the Hotel over to a bright, energetic team, headed by Carl G. Thurston. Thurston, a Roanoke native and a career hotel man, returned to his hometown to fulfill a dream of many years. When he heard the call from Hotel Roanoke, he was manager of the Hilton Hawaiian Village, at that time the world's largest resort hotel. He had also been manager of the Waldorf-Astoria Hotel in New York. Another member of the new management team was Fred Walker, also a Virginian, who had come to the Hotel as director of sales from the Hotel Chamberlin in Hampton, Virginia, and who would in time become general manager himself. With them in the front office and providing continuity with the past was Janet Jenkins, who, having come to the

OPPOSITE, TOP Ken Wilkey shows off the new (1963) Whistle Stop, the Hotel's highly successful watering hole. *Courtesy of the Historical Society of Western Virginia.*

OPPOSITE, BOTTOM The Motor Inn, located in the east wing, opened in 1963. It was not a success and, in due course, closed. *Courtesy of the Historical Society of Western Virginia.*

Hotel in 1950 as a part-time secretary, became its general manager in 1976. It was she who has described the major players of the time: Denison was "a cultured gentleman who never lost his temper," Thurston was "a man of almost aristocratic bearing, with many ideas and a great flair for promotion," and Walker was "outgoing and generous with his time." Still to come was Ken Wilkey, brilliant and innovative, who followed Walker as general manager in 1971. All of these, in their own way and following their own skills and talents, like their predecessors and successors, left memorable marks on the Hotel and its image.

The Motor Inn was Walker's idea, and its addition to the Hotel, like Thurston's swimming pool, was virtually obligatory if the Hotel was to remain competitive. Just as it could be argued that the interstate highway system played a big part in the demise of railway passenger business, it can be argued with equal cogency that it didn't do much to help downtown hotels either. Hotel Roanoke caught it both ways. In the battle between trains and interstates, the *Is* clearly had it.

In this connection, the observations of George Ruff, who saw the victory, are instructive. In the 1950s, he was Norfolk and Western's traveling passenger agent, a job title now as antique as "cordwainer." He was based in Memphis and covered Tennessee, Arkansas, Texas, Oklahoma, New Mexico and Arizona. One part of his job was to solicit businesses and associations to plan their meetings and conventions at Hotel Roanoke and, while they were at it, to route themselves over Norfolk and Western tracks to get there. In many cases, the people he dealt with had memories of happy times spent at the Hotel, and this, he wrote later, "provided a great entree for a presentation." Such presentations frequently turned out to be profitable, as when one customer chartered a train to Roanoke and its Hotel. The president of a banking association in a western state routed his special train over NW tracks whenever possible; a traffic officer of a grain company wanted the pattern number and producer of the Hotel's distinctive dogwood china for his wife. Ruff later wrote, almost in amazement, that "it was difficult to understand how so many people in widely diverse parts of the country far removed from Roanoke could be so familiar with the Hotel."

Another source of potential passenger traffic—and Hotel occupancy—was the flow of students to and from Virginia's colleges and universities, especially those reasonably close to Roanoke: Roanoke College, Hollins College, Radford University, Longwood College (both known by other names in the days of which Ruff speaks), Virginia Tech, Washington and Lee University, Virginia Military Institute, Sweetbriar College

OPPOSITE Two billboards, the top from 1938, proclaim the Hotel's new air-conditioned status; the second is from a few years earlier, possibly the late 1920s. *Courtesy of N&W Photo, K.L. Miller Collection.*

and Randolph-Macon Woman's College, among others. Ruff got the names and addresses of new and returning students from the colleges' admissions offices and, so equipped, found it easy to suggest to the parents that they deliver their children to college personally, and while they're in the neighborhood, why, just stay at the Hotel Roanoke for a couple of days before taking NW's No. 3 west and home. Ruff discovered that often one parent or the other had a connection of some sort with their sons' and daughters' schools and already felt strong ties to them—and the Hotel.

Then after a bit, things changed, for the very people who formerly piled aboard a train and checked their trunks, golf clubs and tennis racquets ahead now found it easier and cheaper to load it all in a station wagon, somehow insert the student and maybe a sibling or two and spend a couple of nights en route at the proliferating motels. By then, these multistoried buildings with their casual dining rooms, perhaps a bar, free breakfast or at least free coffee and doughnuts, swimming pools and individual private room entrances with parking spots right in front had come a long way from earlier "tourist courts" and "tourist cabins" of dreary appearance and even drearier repute. Why, reasoned the driver of a car loaded with children and luggage, should we drive downtown looking for a hotel when we had just passed a sign that read "Holiday Inn—Next Exit"? For many, these go-to-college, return-from-college expeditions took on the air of an enjoyable little family vacation.

So the traveling public not only got off the trains, but they checked out of the downtown hotels as well. Even Hotel Roanoke, with a solid convention business and a small but solid core of patrons, was not immune from the general exodus. The Hotel tried to recapture some of its lost trade by borrowing the fundamental convenience appeal of its highway-side competition and wedding it to its own traditions of comfort and excellence. Thus, in creating a Motor Inn in 1963, the Hotel was in fact following a national trend. *The Hospitality Industry in the United States* (Paul R. Dittmer and Gerald G. Griffin, Van Nostrand Reinhold, 1993) noted that "established center-city hotels, many of them near disused railroad terminals…were becoming ever more costly to maintain.…Most were threatened with loss of business to the new booming motel industry.…Many…began to call themselves motor hotels or motor inns to suggest that the automobile traveler would be as satisfied in these accommodations as he was in a motel."

Hotel Roanoke's Motor Inn was set up with its own desk staff in the wing on the northeast side facing the railroad's Roanoke Shops. A new entrance was created, with its own canopy—which echoed the spirit but not the substance of the awning at the

OPPOSITE   Once, in the 1960s, a livestock association staged a cattle auction in the ballroom (the floor of which was suitably protected); in a very few hours, the same space was cleaned, deodorized and set up for a Roanoke Symphony Ball. *Courtesy of Special Collections, University Libraries, Virginia Tech.*

Hotel's main entrance on the other side of the sprawling building. It extended down the stairway that led to a parking spot for registering guests.

Alas, though Denison had proclaimed that "guests will be afforded all the convenience of a motel combined with the charm and comfort of a major hostelry," the Motor Inn's appeal was not large and its patronage less, especially in view of the slick motel competition in the valley. Further, it was expensive to operate because it required three desk shifts each day, a cost not supported by revenue. It turned out to be a failed experiment, limped along for a few short years and then, with significantly less fanfare than attended its opening, quietly went out of business in the mid-1960s.

Such changes and improvements, steady and costly, were undertaken to make the Hotel, along with its ambiance, cuisine and other trappings, more attractive, especially to business meetings. Soliciting and landing such business was traditionally the prime concern of the Hotel's general managers. From Ken Hyde and George Denison through Carl Thurston, Fred Walker, Ken Wilkey, Janet Jenkins, Peter Kipp and Doreen Hamilton Fishwick, each lent a particular talent and even genius to the goal of expanding the occupancy rate and filling the Regency Room. Hotel Roanoke thought its best convention market lay within a day's drive—in Virginia first, then neighboring states and then the remaining Mid-Atlantic states. Such national conventions that came its way were mainly the outgrowth of local or regional organizations with national ties.

The convention business was eminently worth pursuing. The International Association of Convention and Visitors Bureaus reported that in 1987, just two years before the Hotel dosed, there had been nearly 200,000 business meetings nationally, attended by 68.4 million persons, who spent $37.5 billion in the process. It was a large cash melon to dip a spoon into and explains why Hotel Roanoke management devoted much of its energy to it. When Janet Jenkins retired as general manager in 1980, she had firmly or tentatively booked conventions as far ahead as 1990. When the Hotel closed, one of the terminal chores was to cancel meetings scheduled well into the '90s.

Sales and promotional efforts, including the films, personal calls by the Hotel staff in cooperation with an energetic group in the Roanoke Chamber of Commerce, became highly successful. Some organizations never met anywhere else but the Hotel,

OPPOSITE, TOP One of the Hotel's regular big events was the Norfolk and Western Railway's Annual Better Service Conference. These are the attendees at the 1952 meeting. *Courtesy of N&W Photo, K.L. Miller Collection.*

OPPOSITE, BOTTOM A banquet event for Lions Club members and NW employees, April 1932. *Courtesy of N&W Photo, K.L. Miller Collection.*

Banquet Lions Club and N&W - Hotel Roanoke - April 1932

and others returned if not annually then at least on a regular schedule. The Virginia Pharmaceutical Association came every two or three years. Robert A. Garland, a longtime association member and former Roanoke city councilman, has said that the VPA's membership "felt that the Hotel Roanoke was far superior to its competition in other parts of the state and preferred it." He attended these meetings both as a member and as a child, when his father, a pharmacist, would bring him along.

The Virginias-Carolinas Hospital Association was another regular in the Hotel. It was always the biggest, counting up to 1,200 attendees. Though the Hotel could not accommodate that many guests—other city hotels took the overflow—Hotel Roanoke was the site of the business sessions and exhibits. It may be, of course, that films and sales talk persuaded such institutions to come to the Hotel, but it seems clear that what brought them back time and again was the Hotel itself—its facilities, style, service, menu and, above all, people.

An outstanding example of the Hotel's appeal is the experience of Moore's, the nine-state building materials chain. It held its first sales meeting in the Hotel in 1987, the second in 1988, the third in 1989 and had scheduled its fourth for 1990. The company came back because, in the words of Jim Boutilier, Moore's vice president of human resources, "they [the Hotel] have what we need," and cited events in the 1988 meeting. That year, Moore's, bringing in 350 people from seventy-five stores and headquarters, required registration facilities, a total of six meals, plus two receptions, three refreshment breaks and two entertainment programs, each demanding its own lighting and sound needs, and of course, general meeting sessions and group seminars, plus the appropriate number of guest rooms and suites.

To accommodate all of this, which had been planned for months, Charlotte Facella, the Hotel's sales manager at the time, set aside the ballroom and Shenandoah Room for the large meetings, meals, parties and entertainment. Half of the Exhibit Hall was devoted to signage, display materials and displays, and the other half had video games and pool tables for attendees' relaxation; the Core Room, tools and hardware; the Pocahontas-Cavalier Rooms, kitchen displays; the Pine Room, outdoor grills and lawnmowers; and the Oval Room, mini-computers and registration.

Each detail was written down long before the first chair was set up in the ballroom, the first napkin folded in the Regency Room. Close connections among the Hotel's departments—sales, catering, housekeeping, engineering, security—were absolutely essential. A coffee break ten minutes late, a burned-out bulb in a slide projector, a defective sound system could mean a spoiled meeting for the client and lost future business for the Hotel.

For Moore's, "there [was] responsiveness and enthusiasm for our meeting," Boutilier has said. "And professionalism. I saw a lot of professionalism over there."

Beyond the smooth running, beyond the high level of excellence, however, Moore's found a human side to the Hotel. "One of the men attending the [1988] meeting was in a major health situation, in need of a kidney transplant. We had told the Hotel staff about it; so when at 10:10 one morning we learned that a kidney had become available in Pennsylvania, the Hotel switchboard was able to locate our man and helped us charter a plane to take him to Pennsylvania. Another example: one of our blind employees was attending and for him, as for the kidney patient, the Hotel made special efforts. That's what I mean by professionalism, and nice people. We had great experience at Hotel Roanoke."

Clearly, not all of Hotel Roanoke's meetings were as elaborate as Moore's, but many were larger. Five hundred attendees was an easily manageable number, which also left ample space for a smaller meeting or two as well as for individual guests.

An undated piece of puffery from the Hotel makes an interesting observation: "We serve approximately 175 conventions annually—sometimes three at a time— and anyone attending all meetings there would have considerably more than a liberal education. He would learn about nursing, mathematics, metal health, railroad signals, candy merchandising, embalming, apple blight, sorority customs, maritime law and about every other item in the encyclopedia."

Conventions, whatever their content or size, were not always fully appreciated by other guests. On one occasion, a woman who was holding her daughter's wedding reception in the Shenandoah Room at the end of Peacock Alley came to Billy Davis, the assistant banquet manager, in a highly upset condition. The problem, she explained, was that guests coming to the reception had to pass a display of caskets set up in Peacock Alley for a meeting of state morticians. It was all very upsetting and inappropriate on this happy occasion. Could something be done perhaps to remove them, she wanted to know. Alas, no ma'am, I am afraid not, was the courteous but unchangeable answer.

Weddings and receptions were a major part of locally generated business, involving, according to size, the Pine Room, the Shenandoah Room and even the ballroom for really large parties. Billy Davis said he had handled so many weddings and receptions in his job as assistant banquet manager that he could virtually "cry on request." And yet, with all that, there was once even a funeral at the Hotel. Clearly not as joyful an occasion as the weddings, it nevertheless reflected the mystical, familial, personal hold the Hotel exerted on its guests.

Mrs. Ava Scott, a Roanoke music teacher, had retired and moved to Florida. Yet every year she would return to Roanoke and spend several weeks of the summer in the Hotel. One year, she became very ill and had to return home to Florida, where she died. Her daughter told Janet Jenkins that Mrs. Scott, in her last years, had specified

cremation and that her ashes be spread over the Hotel's grounds. After a review with appropriate city officials, this last guest request was granted. While Mrs. Scott's ashes were being scattered under a large magnolia on the Hotel's lawn by her daughter and a clergyman, Mrs. Jenkins was delivering a eulogy in Parlor D to a group of Mrs. Scott's friends. It was, she has said, "a touching and terrible experience, because I was very emotional."

Celebrating and grieving families aside, Hotel Roanoke had many allies in its steady efforts to fill the rooms. One was the railroad itself, which from the very beginning and by whatever name enjoyed with the Hotel "a mutually advantageous arrangement," as one anonymous Hotel officer put it. The railroad's board of directors met there regularly, the annual shareholders' meeting was held in the Crystal Ballroom (at which vast numbers of the Hotel's justly famous ham biscuits were consumed) and the special NW shareholders meeting in which the consolidation with Southern Railway

ABOVE The Hotel and its grounds in 1941. *Courtesy of N&W Photo, K.L. Miller Collection.*

was approved (in only four minutes) in the Shenandoah Room. Executives brought guests to lunch and dinner. Among them was the Japanese ambassador to the United States, touring railroad facilities, for Japan was for many years the principal export destination for NW-hauled coal. William B. Bales, who later became the railroad's vice president for coal marketing, recalled that he was invited to lunch there by Vice President Thomas Hamill as part of Bales's job interview. "I was thoroughly impressed and my ego inflated considerably." In later years, "we had visitors from Japan and most countries in Europe and South America, and we always went to the Hotel for lunch or dinner. I would watch them taste peanut soup for the first time and sensed that they were not quite sure what they were eating—although everyone seemed to enjoy this special treat." Lawrence Forbes, a former Virginian Railway officer and, after that line's merger with the Norfolk and Western, one of Bales's predecessors as senior coal marketing officer, has a similar recollection: "I thought of the Hotel as a showplace for our foreign and domestic coal buyers. We always received raves about the grits and Virginia ham and peanut soup."

The railroad's principal and largest meeting in the Hotel for many years was the Annual Better Service Conference, requiring many of the Hotel's guest and meeting rooms for its sessions. This brought to the Hotel hundreds of employees from all levels for two or three days of earnest discussions on the paramount issue of providing better service to its customers. Various committees met for what are now called "break-out sessions" to hammer out ideas and suggestions and prepare reports. These were delivered in front of the entire group in the Crystal Ballroom.

It was here during the 1948 conference that the late Richard F. Dunlap was required to deliver his committee's report. Dunlap was a native Roanoker and recalled being taken at the age of ten to the Hotel after church for Sunday dinner. He had earned medals for valor and wounds as an infantry officer in New Guinea during World War II; in 1948, back on the railroad, he was assistant roadmaster in Crewe. He stood up to face not only six hundred of his fellow railroaders but President R.H. Smith, a formidable presence, as well. Recalling the incident forty-five years later, he said, "My knees were knocking, and I was sweating from armpit to belt buckle. I knew if I messed this up, I would be an assistant roadmaster for life." Since he subsequently became Norfolk and Western's president in the course of a career in which timidity was conspicuously absent, readers may safely assume he did not "mess up" his report.

The railroad was also a major tenant at one time. It occurred shortly after the failure of the Motor Inn experiment, when the railroad was in the process of bringing new life into its piggyback, or intermodal, section, which then as now involved the movement of highway trailers and containers on railroad flat cars. To develop and exploit this promising line of business, R.B. Short ("Reggie" to all, "Shorty" to some)

was brought in from St. Louis, where this certified original had worked for the old Wabash Railroad. In Roanoke, he found that there was no room in the General Office Building for his growing department. He looked at and rejected possible space in the railroad's garage behind the Hotel.

One day, late in 1967, along with Herman Pevler, Norfolk and Western's president (for whom Short had worked on the Wabash), and Richard Dunlap, then NW's vice president for operations, Reggie toured the former—and now empty—Motor Inn space. As Short recalls, the dialogue on the tour ran roughly like this:

Pevler: "How would this do?"

Short: "Looks perfect."

Pevler (to Dunlap): "Draw up the plans."

OPPOSITE At work in the new kitchen, 1938. *Courtesy of the Historical Society of Western Virginia.*

ABOVE Kylene Barker, the first Miss Virginia to become Miss America, was honored in 1978 when the Hotel hung her portrait in Peacock Alley. Miss Barker, holding flowers, seems pleased. *Courtesy of the Historical Society of Western Virginia.*

The plans, when drawn and executed, called for tearing out some walls and fixtures to create space sufficiently large to accommodate Short's forty intermodalists. They kept the Motor Inn canopy and had to themselves the entire first floor, which Larry Keoughan, one of the flock, remembered later as having none of the distractions found elsewhere—meaning drop-in visits—and was thus "most conducive to working."

Reggie Short had a friend build for him a downsized version of a highway trailer's back door and had it installed as the entrance to his department's offices.

What befell Hotel Roanoke's traditional décor after that has been described by Frank Wilner, a Short underling at the time (later a vice president of the Association of American Railroads) who has referred to Short as a "mercurial marketing magician."

"This [the trailer door]," he wrote, "was not sufficient to the decorating needs of Mr. Short. He demanded of each of his employees the attitude of a hungry tiger. So he ordered that the walls of his Intermodal Department be painted a burnt orange! And they were. And for months afterward, most employees left their daily labors with splitting headaches from the abusive glare that instigated not a few verbal arguments."

Without apology—in fact, with something approaching pride—Short has cheerfully defended his decorating taste: his department's space was widely known as "Shorty's pumpkin." "In any case, we had good fun over there. We had good people. We were close to the Regency Room and the Pickwick Club, and that impressed customers. We stayed busy taking customers away from the Chessie and the Pennsy. We made a few bucks, too."

And spent them. As tenants, even though railroad tenants, Short's department paid rent, which included, it should be noted, fresh-wrapped soap supplied by maid service every night. Janet Jenkins quotes fondly the Hotel's traditional rule: "There are no freebies. The NW pays its way, but it knows it's getting its money's worth in service." Even fresh-wrapped soap.

The railroad's presidents were frequent visitors. Or not, according to Mrs. Jenkins, who saw several of them. R.H. "Race Horse" Smith was a fairly infrequent visitor. He "ran in like a racehorse to see Mr. Denison from time to time." Although she saw him on those occasions, he had no small talk beyond a "good morning." W.J. Jenks had lunch at the Hotel every day and was served for dessert very thin cookies, made only for him and him alone. Stuart Saunders, founder of the modern merger movement among American railroads, would sometimes arrive "followed by a small retinue" and declare he wanted a meeting room right away. "Someone would make faces at me over his shoulder in an attempt to make me laugh," she recalls. And did she? "Not that I recall."

Herman Pevler was "a great and good friend." When his election to the railroad's presidency was announced, the newspaper published a photograph showing his shock

TOP The property's north courtyard, serving as the Conference Center's main entrance, employs rectangular flower beds that recall in their shapes the flower beds of the previous 1938 formal garden. *Courtesy of Hotel Roanoke.*

BOTTOM The Conference Center of Roanoke, an International Association of Conference Centers–approved space, adjoins the Hotel Roanoke & Conference Center and offers a combined sixty-three thousand square feet of flexible meeting space and thirty-five meeting rooms. *Courtesy of Hotel Roanoke.*

ABOVE Listed in the National Register of Historic Places, Hotel Roanoke offers sophisticated style and comfortable accommodations in Virginia's gorgeous mountain landscape. *Courtesy of Hotel Roanoke.*

OPPOSITE The Honorable Bob Goodlatte commemorated the Hotel Roanoke & Conference Center in his final term, recognizing the historic hotel on its 136th anniversary and its contributions to the region and state. *Courtesy of Hotel Roanoke.*

RECOGNIZING THE 136TH ANNIVERSARY OF THE HOTEL ROANOKE & CONFERENCE CENTER

HON. BOB GOODLATTE

OF VIRGINIA

IN THE HOUSE OF REPRESENTATIVES

Monday, December 17, 2018

Mr. GOODLATTE. Mr. Speaker, I am happy to recognize a National Historic Landmark located in my hometown of Roanoke, Virginia in the Sixth Congressional District. The Hotel Roanoke & Conference Center stands at the heart of Roanoke's downtown, on a hill in the Gainsboro neighborhood where it has been located for 136 years.

Roanoke was founded as the confluence of two railroads. The Norfolk and Western Railway established the city as its hub. The N&W – now Norfolk Southern – constructed the Hotel Roanoke and opened it on Christmas Day 1882. Since then, it has welcomed men, women, and children from all walks of life to enjoy the hotel's lodging, its amenities – including its Southern cuisine, like its famous peanut soup – and just the chance to spend time in one of the city's cultural centers.

Regretfully, due to declining interest in maintaining the historic structure, the Hotel Roanoke closed on November 30, 1989. The contents of the hotel were even sold to interested buyers. Fortunately, thanks to an agreement with Virginia Tech and the desire of community leaders to redevelop the dilapidated structure, more than 2,800 people and businesses pledged the funds needed to help the Renew Roanoke effort, which raised $8 million to save the hotel from demolition.

In a partnership that included the Virginia Tech Real Estate Foundation and the City of Roanoke, the completely renovated Hotel Roanoke & Conference Center opened in April 1995. The city built a pedestrian bridge to connect the facility to the central business district, a vital connection that has contributed heavily to the rebirth of Roanoke's downtown. It's estimated in the 23 years since its reopening, the hotel and conference center has had a $558 million economic impact and has led to hundreds of millions of dollars in additional investments by a wide variety of housing interests, businesses, restaurants, and cultural amenities.

Affiliated as a Doubletree hotel from its reopening, the Hotel Roanoke & Conference recently converted to Hilton's Curio Collection. It's the latest update to take the structure known for its Tudor-style construction into a new role in Roanoke's growth. I've been blessed to enjoy countless happy occasions with family members and friends at "the Grand Old Lady on the Hill." The Hotel Roanoke's 136th anniversary is just a week away. It's a fine time to celebrate not only the Christmas holidays but the contributions made by the Hotel Roanoke to the region's history and its very promising future.

Hotel Roanoke, Roanoke, Va.

OPPOSITE, TOP Hotel Roanoke, in an almost constant state of growth and change since the 1880s, today retains wings from several construction periods, each with subtle variations in the use and placement of materials and ornamental details. *Terry Aldhizer Photography.*

OPPOSITE, BOTTOM This 1910 image shows the Hotel with its expansive grounds, which were part of the attraction of the Hotel for guests. *Nelson Harris collection.*

TOP This 1905 postcard shows the NW Railway passenger station at left and the railroad's general office building in center background. *Nelson Harris collection.*

MIDDLE The Hotel's location on a prominent knoll within sight of downtown has made it the city's signature structure for over a century. *Nelson Harris collection.*

BOTTOM This postcard shows much of the Hotel's south wing, a vast improvement in accommodations over the Hotel's original thirty-four guest rooms in 1882. *Nelson Harris collection.*

Hotel Roanoke, Roanoke, Va.

OPPOSITE, TOP LEFT   The main entrance to the Hotel with its circular drive was part of the redesign that occurred in the late 1930s. *Nelson Harris collection.*

OPPOSITE, TOP RIGHT   This 1950s aerial view card shows the Hotel's proximity to the American Legion Auditorium, *upper right*, which was Roanoke's primary entertainment venue at that time. *Nelson Harris collection.*

OPPOSITE, MIDDLE   This postcard from the 1950s shows the Hotel following post–World War II expansion and renovations. *Nelson Harris collection.*

OPPOSITE, BOTTOM   This night-view postcard dates to the 1950s. The Hotel hosted the Miss Virginia pageant for the first time in 1954. *Nelson Harris collection.*

TOP   The Hotel was originally designed in the Queen Anne style by its Philadelphia architect, George Pearson. The design style never deviated over the years. *Nelson Harris collection.*

BOTTOM   This 1930s postcard shows the stone wall, an intended design element, which encircled the Hotel grounds with pillars at main entry points. *Nelson Harris collection.*

OPPOSITE   Set in the Roanoke Valley and surrounded by the Blue Ridge Mountains, the Hotel Roanoke & Conference Center offers a scenic location and easy access to hiking, boating and fishing. *Courtesy of Brian Wells.*

ABOVE   From grand events and famous Sunday brunches to halls of glorious Christmas trees, the Hotel Roanoke is not only a destination for visitors but also a crown jewel for residents of Roanoke and Virginia's Blue Ridge. *Courtesy of Brian Wells.*

TOP The Regency Room and the Pine Room Pub are the perfect place to enjoy dinner or drinks on the patio, offering spectacular views of downtown Roanoke and Mill Mountain. *Courtesy of Brian Wells.*

BOTTOM From the antique-filled lobby to the surrounding decor, guests will find a unique blend of historic charm and modern comforts when visiting the historic property. *Courtesy of Brian Wells.*

OPPOSITE, TOP The Crystal Ballroom is the quintessential setting for your dream wedding or other formal ceremony. Serving as an illustrious backdrop for romance and a breathtaking setting for lavish celebrations that offers plenty of amenities, the ballroom is one of two grand ballrooms at the Hotel Roanoke & Conference Center. *Courtesy of Brian Wells.*

OPPOSITE, BOTTOM Enjoy a memorable stay at the Hotel Roanoke & Conference Center, Curio Collection by Hilton. Built in 1882, this historic hotel is rich in tradition and charm, from the rocking chairs at the entrance to the murals on the walls and all the smaller details in between. *Courtesy of Brian Wells.*

ABOVE Some of the Hotel's guests have included presidents of the United States (such as Jimmy Carter, pictured here fourth from left), governors, millionaires, theater and sports stars, attendees for political and business conventions and Miss Virginia competitors since 1953. Not as celebrated as these notables but perhaps more important—since they have always formed the core of the Hotel's business—are countless thousands of Roanokers. *Courtesy of Brian Wells.*

OPPOSITE, TOP Guests are greeted in the lobby by the mural scenes, researched and executed by artist Hugo Ohlms. The scenes include *The Landing at Jamestown, 1607*; *Baptism of Pocahontas*; *Marriage of Pocahontas*; *The First Representative Government in America, 1619*; *The Surrender of Lord Cornwallis at Yorktown, 1781*; *William and Mary College*; *Patrick Henry's Address, 1765*; *Women Arrive at Jamestown, 1619*; and *Virginia Hospitality*. *Courtesy of Hotel Roanoke.*

OPPOSITE, MIDDLE The lobby of Hotel Roanoke when affiliated as a Doubletree hotel. *Courtesy of Hotel Roanoke.*

OPPOSITE, BOTTOM Within the north lobby, adjacent to Wells Avenue, hang the three magnificent Czechoslovakian crystal chandeliers from which the Crystal Ballroom took its name. *Courtesy of Hotel Roanoke.*

ABOVE The newly renovated seasonal outdoor swimming pool and year-round whirlpool provide great scenery for relaxation or a quick bite to eat while visiting. *Courtesy of Hotel Roanoke.*

OPPOSITE, TOP Peacock Alley extends northward from the Palm Court toward the meeting rooms at the north end of the main building. The paneled walls and covered ceiling of the long corridor are highlighted by three triptych sets of hand-blocked English wallpaper panels featuring peacocks perched amid lush garden foliage. *Courtesy of Hotel Roanoke.*

OPPOSITE, BOTTOM Fluted Doric columns and pilasters mark the location of the Palm Court, originally known as the Oval Room and later as the Colonial Room. The large oval space serves as an important circulation route, as it links the Main Lobby with the Pine Room, Peacock Alley and the East Wing; it also serves as a well-defined gathering space. *Courtesy of Hotel Roanoke.*

A small private dining room, the Virginia Room, is located just off the main dining room in a unique octagonal space defined by the southwest corner tower. The Virginia Room features floor-to-ceiling knotty pine paneling, a paneled plaster ceiling and a dramatic brass and crystal chandelier and dogwood-pattern wall sconces. *Courtesy of Hotel Roanoke.*

of white hair. Soon after, a man came in wearing a hat, asking to see Fred Walker, the manager. "And whom shall I say..." began Mrs. Jenkins. "Pevler," he growled and removed his hat to provide further identification.

When, in April 1970, Pevler retired as president, he took office space in the Hotel on the floor just above the executive offices. Sharing the three-room suite with him were Jesse Gearhart, who had been on the presidential staff, and later Fred Walker, who had moved from the Hotel's general managership to become public affairs director of the Virginia Holding Company, another NW subsidiary. After Pevler's death, his widow told Mrs. Jenkins that he had wanted her to have his old desk—the same one, Gearhart believes, he had used as president of the Wabash Railroad. (Eventually, the desk ended up in the Norfolk office of the chairman of Norfolk Southern Corporation, David R. Goode.)

Close behind the railroad itself as a major source of business was the chamber of commerce and its offspring, the Roanoke Valley Convention and Visitors Bureau. The dynamic Jack Smith, who headed the chamber for many years, roamed far over the commonwealth, sometimes accompanied by Fred Walker, talking to organizations about meeting at Hotel Roanoke and often delivering his sales pitch directly to sitting conventions. Working with him on this ongoing effort were Jack Goodykoontz, John Kelley and Margaret Baker, making up what Janet Jenkins has called "a great team." "They knew that the city would share in whatever prosperity Hotel Roanoke enjoyed." Elizabeth Bowles, though not an official of the chamber, and the chamber's Smith and Baker were major players in the association of the Miss Virginia pageant with Hotel Roanoke, in bringing it to the Hotel and in keeping it there. Bowles as a member of Roanoke's Junior Woman's Club helped obtain for Roanoke the available Miss Virginia franchise from the Miss America Pageant's famous Leonore Slaughter, beginning in 1953. A decade later, faced with the possible loss of the franchise, the ubiquitous Smith formed a nonprofit organization (Miss Virginia Pageant Inc.) to retain it for the Hotel and city. Directors were Horace Fitzpatrick, Robert Lynn, Barton Morris, John Butler, Richard Edwards and the Hotel's own Fred Walker.

The actual pageant ceremonies were held in other places in the city, but the Hotel became the pageant's headquarters, and the substantial business it brought in was especially welcome since it took place typically in July, the slow season. The house was filled with the contestants and accompanying chaperones (only their rooms were complimentary), families, friends, sponsors, volunteers and media folk. The pageant for many years was a major community event, with a parade and bands and the contestants in long dresses and gloves riding along perched on the back seats of new convertibles provided by Roanoke's auto dealers.

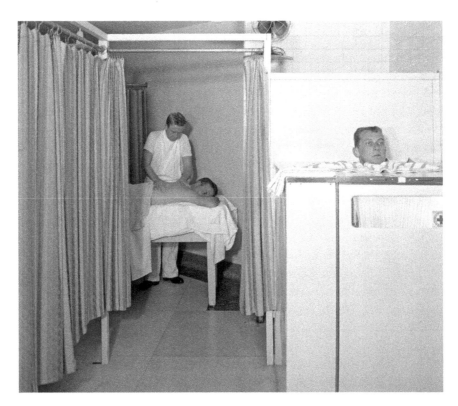

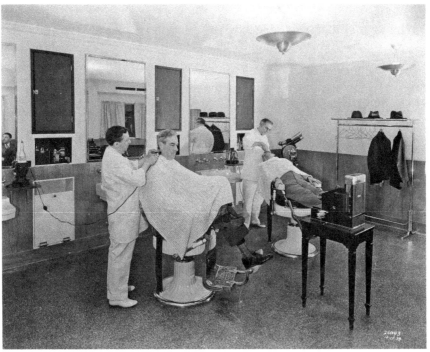

Guests take advantage of the numerous amenities at Hotel Roanoke. *Opposite, top: Courtesy of Norfolk Southern Corporation; opposite, bottom: courtesy of Special Collections, University Libraries, Virginia Tech; above: courtesy of Norfolk Southern Corporation.*

Each new Miss Virginia had the use of a suite in the Hotel for the year of her celebrity. Kylene Barker, the only Miss Virginia (1978) to go on to become Miss America, got a further special distinction from the Hotel—a suite bearing her name. (It had been the John Randolph Suite, and a less likely pairing of the beauty queen and the irascible Virginian cannot be imagined. He was hot-tempered and a formidable hater. He once thrashed a fellow congressman with his cane and compared another to a dead mackerel in the moonlight: "brilliant but stinking.") Barker has declared that the Hotel "changed my life. It was the grandest hotel I'd ever seen...a quiet elegance that was hard to find elsewhere....[As Miss America] I had the opportunity...to stay in the most beautiful hotels, but hardly any of them could hold a candle to Hotel Roanoke."

She wrote a book, *Southern Beauty*, in 1984. "Even though it was a book to promote good diet, exercise, etc., I couldn't help but include the Hotel's recipe for Peanut Soup." *People* magazine's critic didn't like the book, she says, "but loved the recipe."

Through the pageant, the city and the Hotel derived considerable publicity, with well-known judges (one of whom thought spoonbread was a dessert). Every one of the Hotel's managers, reports Margaret Baker, who worked with them all from the mid-1950s, "was delighted to have the pageant. Doreen Hamilton Fishwick was especially good to us. Whatever we needed—within reason, anyway—she did for us. She said more than once that the pageant is good for us, for you and the whole valley."

RIGHT Norfolk and Western Railway's Annual Better Service Meeting, April 2, 1948. *Courtesy of N&W Photo, K.L. Miller Collection.*

Taking the same line was Bowles, who later served on Roanoke City Council. "The pageant brought us notice and prestige, since localities with contestants sent their own reporters; and in later years, the pageant was televised statewide." She recalls that after the pageant, there was always a big party in the ballroom for the sponsors, volunteers and contributors; but "under the rules in those days, the competitors couldn't be in attendance at parties where alcohol was served, so we arranged for them to have pizza parties in the Pine Room."

(Bowles also had a personal part in bringing another sort of group to the Hotel: the reunion of the 106th Infantry Division, in which her husband served in the Second World War. At the division's reunion in South Carolina in 1993, many asked when they would come back to "that grand Hotel." She also had a hand in bringing a state convention of ex–prisoners of war to the Hotel.)

For Misses Virginia, Hotel Roanoke was so much of a part of their lives that Margaret Baker says one former titleholder returned to Roanoke for a visit, and when she saw the Hotel was closed, she "burst into tears."

The chamber itself used the Hotel facilities for out-of-town guests, for seminars and meetings and, most notably, for its annual dinner meeting. Michael Ramsey, at the time a staff member, attended the 1981 meeting, his first black-tie event in Roanoke.

"Actually, only those of us on the dais wore black ties; the mostly male audience was in business attire, some obviously selected by their wives. The ambiance was inspiring… the chicken cordon bleu, a house wine not too disagreeable. I was impressed by how easily Billy and Alex seemed to orchestrate the staff without much of a fuss."

At a later dinner, the chamber's membership-raising arm, the Backbone Club, was relegated to the Pine Room for lack of space in the ballroom and had to watch the proceedings there on closed circuit television. Says Ramsey, "The Backboners were more exuberant than usual. It was a 'spirited' evening; the food-to-liquid ratio changing appreciably during the meal.…The dessert was a banquet concoction topped with dollops of hard meringue which it was learned could be flung a far distance when propelled by a dessert spoon.…That was the last time the Backbone Club was ever separated from the rest of the dinner guests."

The funds spent on the Hotel over the years increased its attractiveness to guests, not merely in the regular cycle of room redecorating, but in facilities as well. Traditionally, the Hotel had provided good taste, elegance, even serenity, a combination Janet Jenkins has labeled "a little luxury for an economical price." As competition grew in the interstate highway/motel world, more was needed, simply because the traveling public—and the ever-growing size of the conventioning public—demanded it.

So there came the swimming pool in 1962, where Farnham's tulip garden had been planted nearly thirty-five years before. Later, a roof made year-round swimming possible, and Carl Thurston created a sun-and-fun club so Roanokers could enjoy the same relaxation as guests; even later, there was also poolside meal service and nighttime dancing.

There was the Pickwick Club, a private eating-and-drinking establishment in the days before the state's liquor laws were changed to permit the sale of alcoholic beverages by the drink. It was handsomely furnished in a comfortable English style with period antiques and had its own kitchen and staff, separate from the Hotel in every respect but location. The club also had the only working fireplace ever constructed in the Hotel (at least, since the "bar-rooms" in the original Hotel building); whimsical at best, it was seldom used. (One of its early managers kept his books on three-by-five index cards, a fact that created much bemusement on the part of one of the railroad's sophisticated financial officers.) Hotel guests were eligible for a membership that expired upon the guest's departure. The Pickwick Club made no money for the Hotel. When the Hotel eventually needed its space again, the Pickwickians voted to move elsewhere.

There was the Windsor Room, formerly the Coffee Shop, formerly the Fountain Room. "Proper but not stuffy," according to a Hotel publicity piece, its "good-time flair makes it one of Roanoke's most popular nightspots" for dinner and dancing and entertainment. Part of the entertainment was a jazz program on Sunday afternoons. Among the regulars was the Dave Figg Quartet (Dave Figg on tenor sax and his wife, Gene, on piano; Nat Thomas, bass; and Harry Jackson, drums), "plus anybody who cared to sit in." This included Charlie Perkinson, who came to Roanoke in 1970 and soon developed a jazz following for his radio station, WPVR. He would tape the Sunday afternoon program for rebroadcast that same night from the station's studios in the Hotel. (On the station's staff at the time was Adrian Kronauer of *Good Morning Vietnam* renown.)

The Sunday programs typically started at three o'clock and went on two or three hours, and sometimes as late as 7:30 p.m., depending on who was playing and the level of the audience's enthusiasm. The attendance was generally good—"an eclectic group: college students, hotel guests, Roanokers black and white," Perkinson recalls. The Windsor Room later took up rock, and after a while, when interest dropped off, the Windsor Room also shut down.

There was the Ad Lib Club, Peter Kipp's idea for another jazz-and-food place to fill the same site. Done in glitzy red and black, Ad Lib attracted local musicians as well, plus big names from the jazz world: Teddy Wilson, the incomparable pianist who was one of the original members of the Benny Goodman Trio and Quartet; Maxine Sullivan, the singer; and Charlie Byrd, jazz guitarist. Ad Lib was also open for lunch, though without the music. Briefly successful, its appeal eventually faded, the victim of a fickle public.

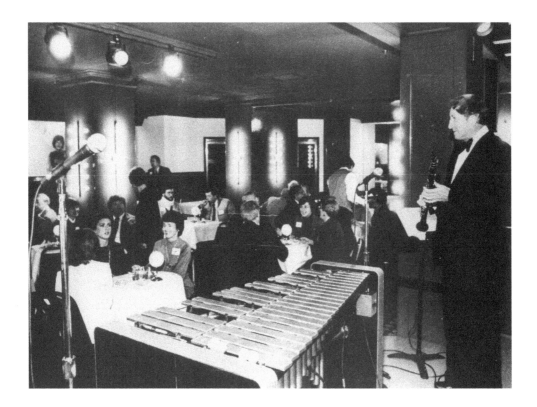

After its demise, Jimmy Butler's Comedy Club settled in, in April 1988, and stayed until the Hotel closed. The club was open Wednesday—the night for local comic talent—through Saturday. Butler paid no rent but took the gate to cover costs and profit and also shared in some receipts. "Business was a ping-pong ball," Butler says.

Ken Wilkey replaced Fred Walker as general manager and came with sound expertise in the food and beverage side of the hotel business. He held a degree in hotel and restaurant management from Oklahoma State University and worked for the Sheraton Corporation, Ramada Inns, Inc. and General Hosts Corporation before coming to Roanoke. He has been described as "brilliant" by Janet Jenkins, and judging from two of his notable innovations in the Hotel, it is an accurate appraisal.

ABOVE Tommy Gwaltney presides over a "preview opening" of the Hotel's Ad Lib Club in November 1987. The club attracted a number of well-known jazz musicians in its all-too-short lifetime. *Courtesy of the Historical Society of Western Virginia.*

Almost immediately after his arrival in 1971, Wilkey set about adding a new style to the Regency Room. Working through Dodie Matze, a Roanoke pianist who occasionally provided music for the diners, Wilkey located and commissioned Joe Corne to create a trio for weekend performances. Corne was a native North Carolinian, holding a master's degree in music from the University of North Carolina; a music teacher, he had also been state table tennis champion for many years and was nationally ranked. Corne came to Roanoke to join the city school system to teach orchestral stringed instruments and, incidentally, to play with groups all over the valley.

When the summons from Wilkey came, Corne already knew a sizable number of musicians from the Coffee Pot, a popular part of the Roanoke music scene, where they frequently played and where he taught them table tennis. With himself on bass; Ron Northrup, classically trained, on the piano; and Sherman Helms on drums, they auditioned and won the job and held it for an astonishing seventeen years. The players varied over that time, drawn from a pool of talent assembled by Corne: pianists Bonnie Todenhoft, Ralph Gravely and Frankie Romano; bassists Lennie Martin, Charlie Perkinson, Nat Paul Thomas and Chuck Cooper; and drummers Morris Elam, Jimmy Lewis and Ronnie Law.

Corne recalls the Regency Room as "a place of glamour. The men were in tuxedos, the women in long dresses. Salads were fixed at the table, and eight dollars bought a first-class dinner. The Windsor Room had excitement with its rock music, but the Regency Room had elegance."

On the first night, the trio themselves wore tuxedos. Although that was not an every-night costume, Corne went through four during his playing years in the Regency Room. The room was full, and the trio began promptly at 7:00 p.m. with a resounding arpeggio from Northrup as an attention-getter and then started in on its menu of show tunes, cocktail music and swing. So successful was the group that after just a month or two Wilkey expanded the contract to include appearances seven nights a week. (It was not until they had been playing at the Hotel for seven years that they got around to naming themselves the Regents, and that was "really just a joke," says Corne apologetically.)

During breaks, Corne would often circulate through the dining room and chat with the patrons, making small talk and accepting requests for songs like the theme from *Dr. Zhivago*, "Moon River," "The Way We Were" and "Send in the Clowns." One evening while roaming the room, he met the film star Donald O'Connor and talked with him about golf and entertainment.

The Regents' last night at the Hotel was November 27, 1989. Gravely, Law and Corne played the theme from *Love Story*, a tune they had played on their first night seventeen years before. "It was a beautiful night," Corne recalls.

Opening day at the Hotel's pool in August 1962 attracted Roanoke mayor Willis Anderson (*at left in bottom picture, opposite*) and interested guests, bystanders and swimmers. *This page*: *courtesy of Norfolk Southern Corporation*; *opposite, top to bottom*: *courtesy of Norfolk Southern Corporation*; *courtesy of Norfolk Southern Corporation*; *courtesy of the Historical Society of Western Virginia.*

The Regents had been playing for five years when Wilkey brought to life the Whistle Stop, an incredibly successful watering hole, serving drink and food in a determinedly railroad atmosphere, a bow to the Hotel's and city's origins.

At that time, Wilkey told the *Norfolk and Western Magazine* that "people seem to be very excited about it. The Hotel needed a place for people to eat that was quiet and moderately priced and this area has provided a happy medium." Wilkey himself undertook to collect much of the memorabilia that decorated the Stop. There were brake sticks, oil cans and shovels from old Norfolk and Western days, a collection of buttons from the uniforms of employees formerly in dining car service, an original poster from 1938 celebrating the railroad's 100th anniversary, lanterns, photographs and a wrought-iron window from the old Christiansburg passenger station's ticket office. As a finishing touch, a sound system was installed so that tapes of train noises could be played for patrons at regular intervals. The Whistle Stop was popular (Senator Charles Robb recalled visiting there with friends for a nightcap) and busy for all its days and nights. Its assortment of railroad memorabilia lent a genuine railroad flavor to the place, which, though lacking the cool elegance of the Regency Room, nevertheless remains a fond memory for thousands of Hotel guests. Like the Comedy Club, the Whistle Stop remained open to the very end, and after the Hotel closed, all of the railroad memorabilia passed to Norfolk Southern.

Chapter 4

LET US NOW PRAISE—OR AT LEAST
TALK ABOUT—FAMOUS PEOPLE

It is generally agreed that John D. Rockefeller—the original John D. Rockefeller—was once a guest of the Hotel. One wishes it to be so, of course. And if so, it raises interesting, if petty, questions. Did he tip the bellman and waiters a shiny dime? Did he pay his bill in shiny dimes? Was he even presented a bill?

In August 1918, three self-described "vagabonds" decided to dine at the Hotel. Having stopped for gas in Roanoke, Henry Ford, Thomas Edison and Harvey Firestone enjoyed a leisurely lunch as chauffeurs refueled their Model Ts.

Never mind if Rockefeller was a guest, he was but one—albeit the richest—of many notables. There were Amelia Earhart and Joe DiMaggio, whose names have also been traditionally associated with the guest registry. Victor Borge, Ethel Merman, a Barrymore or two and others can be considered to be likely because of appearances at the famed and much-lamented Roanoke Academy of Music. Lawrence Tibbett, the great baritone from the Metropolitan Opera, however, is a sure thing, because John Eure, a Roanoke practicing journalist, interviewed him at dinner in the Regency Room on the night of his concert in the old Academy. (Confirming views held by old-line Roanokers, Tibbett told Eure that the Academy had the finest acoustics of any hall he had ever sung in.)

Another concert artist, the pianist Van Cliburn, years later made a lingering impression on the Hotel and its management. While practicing a few hours before his concert, he left the water running in his bathtub, which ultimately overflowed and leaked through the Regency Room ceiling. No one was injured—the diners' peanut soup remained undiluted—but years later, Janet Jenkins still didn't know, despite her instructions, how the piano got above the first floor.

A confirmed sighting is General Dwight D. Eisenhower, who was photographed with Mrs. Eisenhower leaving the Hotel—he with his trademark grin and she with a fussy little hat—after an overnight stop during his term as army chief of staff.

Harry S. Truman stayed at the hotel in 1941 when he was a United States senator representing Missouri.

Billy Sunday, the traditional fire-and-brimstone evangelist, stayed at the Hotel during a six-week crusade in Roanoke. "I have hoped," he declaimed, "for ten years that the Lord would let down the gates to Roanoke and let me in." He told a reporter in his Hotel Roanoke room that "I have preached in Norfolk, Richmond and Bristol and those experiences were just like a Smithfield ham—one taste and you want more." This was in September 1920, long before peanut soup appeared on the Regency Room menu.

Jack Dempsey and Jeanette MacDonald, an unlikely combination, are also recorded guests. The former had been in Roanoke to referee a wrestling match and said of the place in which he spent the night, "That sure is a fine Hotel—one of the best in this part of the country," and spoke of its "remarkable service." Miss MacDonald, "looking very chic in a beige wool traveling frock, mink coat and felt hat trimmed with coq feathers," was in the city to sing a concert in the Roanoke auditorium and stayed in a Hotel suite.

Helen Fitzpatrick, then a reporter, remembers interviewing Carlos R. Romulo during World War II. He was in Roanoke on some now-forgotten mission, a refugee from the Philippines, an associate of General Douglas MacArthur before and during the war. "I was terrified, but he put me at ease, speaking of his family (still in the occupied Philippines) whom he had not heard from. I recall feeling so sad for him, as he did not know if they were dead or alive." (After the war, Romulo became the Philippines ambassador to the United States.)

Philip Sporn, president of American Electric Power Company, meeting at the Hotel one year with his system's managers, had a serious complaint. A man whose intellectual capacity put him at the genius level, he was an inveterate reader, and that, stapled to his electrical background, made him unhappy when he discovered that there were no one-hundred-watt light bulbs in his suite. Bill McClung, Appalachian Power Company's Roanoke man in charge of arrangements, was called on to deal with the matter. Oddly, there were no one-hundred-watt bulbs immediately available, but, McClung has said dryly, "it didn't take long for the housekeeping people to find them." AEP's managers were meeting again at the Hotel when the Northeast blackout of 1967 struck. AEP's utility systems experts were called away immediately from the Roanoke meeting by the Federal Power Commission to help investigate the cause of the widespread calamity and so created a number of vacant rooms in the Hotel.

Celebrities of the Sporn-Romulo-MacDonald stripe aside, it was politics and politicians who were ever drawn to the Hotel, along with all their works and pomps and impedimenta. "Alex" Alexander always liked to see the hue and cry of political conventions, the rallies, breakfasts and receptions in the Hotel, for though they always posed clean-up problems, "the sticks from all the placards and signs made great tomato stakes."

John Eure, indefatigable reporter and pungent observer, met many of the movers, shakers and headliners over the years. One was Alben Barkley, then a senator from Kentucky. Eure took a photographer with him on his interview assignment, but it turned out that there was to be no photo opportunity. Barkley, in his underwear, met Eure at the door to his suite. "He was an amiable Southern gentleman," Eure recalls. "He told jokes, he offered me a drink, and I had a terrible time getting away."

One Sunday afternoon on the Hotel's porch, Eure, as a green reporter, met James Price, a Virginia politician of some stature and nerve—and, as things turned out, prudence. Even though he was not part of the so-called political machine, he had nevertheless built up substantial support and was running for governor, though it was not his ordained turn. To one question, Eure not only didn't get an answer but in fact had to promise not to quote Price as even declining to answer. The result: no story. "I was wholly taken in by this charming politician," Eure confessed.

Senator John Warner, referring to the Hotel as a gathering place for the politicos, has written that "the rocking chairs on the front porch rocked some political careers and made others. I remember many a night falling asleep to the wonderful sounds of passing coal trains." He added that "Hotel Roanoke had the best food and service—it was gracious, traditional Southern hospitality."

Susan Aheron Magell, Warner's chief of staff at the time and a native Roanoker, remembers playing a recital in the Hotel as a first-grade piano student of Mrs. Edgar Foley and being awed by the sight of an older student in a "beautiful, floor-length Scarlett O'Hara dress....I vowed to return when my knees stopped knocking." And she did, for political events involving all three of the political figures for whom she worked: Caldwell Butler, John Dalton and John Warner. (And for her wedding day.)

James Olin remembers the night his wife, Phyllis, came to Roanoke for the first time. He had been recently transferred to Roanoke by General Electric Company. "We were settled down for a good night's sleep on the third floor, when all hell broke loose in the hall and in the rooms on both sides of us. It turned out that the annual convention of the Beta Club sorority was in the Hotel. Those teenagers kept going until three in the morning." Later speaking of his long career as a representative, Olin recalled "the many command performances I attended to explain my voting in Congress." He remembered, too, a "Symphony Ball attended by John Warner, then a candidate for the Senate, and his new wife, Elizabeth Taylor."

For Senator Charles Robb, "the Hotel will always be central to my earlier recollections of the Roanoke Valley....I couldn't count the number of times I stayed there—and even the greater number of times I visited all kinds of conventions, meetings, breakfasts, lunches, dinners....I particularly enjoyed the Hotel's peanut soup and its Sunday brunch." Robb's most memorable visit to the Hotel was in January 1982, when the Roanoke Valley Chamber of Commerce brought eighty members of the Virginia General Assembly via special train to Roanoke for a show-and-beg visit. Scheduled in addition to tours and presentations, there was to be "more than a little partying" and a black-tie dinner dance in the ballroom.

Robert Garland, a veteran political activist, recalls the reception arranged at the Hotel in 1963 by Nelson Rockefeller during his run for the Republican nomination for president. Garland stood in the reception line with Mrs. Rockefeller, and the line of guests reached from the Shenandoah Room down Peacock Alley, through the lobby and out into the parking lot. At the end of the reception, Mrs. Rockefeller, thanking "Shorty" Leftwich for his services as headwaiter, gave him the floral display from the reception's main table.

Counting Rockefeller, there have been five vice presidents of the United States to have stayed at Hotel Roanoke—Spiro Agnew, George Bush, Gerald Ford and Richard Nixon—and three of them became president. Add Ronald Reagan, who visited on political matters when he was governor of California, and Jimmy Carter, who campaigned there for himself.

Agnew's visit as a candidate for vice president on the Republican ticket with Nixon is recalled by Ray Garland, former Virginia state senator and a Republican Party activist. Garland was in charge of the arrangements. "Since Maryland had no lieutenant governor, Agnew still functioned as head of state, and we were told he had to have a direct phone line to Annapolis installed in his suite. That was quite a job and we had to pay for it—several hundred dollars, I think.

"Agnew's family was with him, and we were told his daughters liked to send out for late pizza and we should have a menu available....If they had any Roanoke pizza it is a fact lost to history." Fred Walker says that Agnew—"gracious and charming"— invited him to sit down and chatted about earlier visits to Roanoke, where he said his grandmother had lived.

OPPOSITE, TOP Conference and private dining room. *Courtesy of N&W Photo, K.L. Miller Collection.*

OPPOSITE, BOTTOM Ronald Reagan, when he was governor of California, spoke at the Hotel on behalf of Republican candidates. *Courtesy of the Historical Society of Western Virginia.*

Another telephone, this one red, played a major role in the visit to the Hotel by Vice President Nelson Rockefeller.

Janet Jenkins, the manager, had always said that running a hotel was the ideal job for a woman because it was nothing but running a household, except on a larger scale (this in a period with a less intensive view of gender roles) and "where every guest was treated as a special person." For the visit of the vice president of the United States, a special person by any measure, she played the ultimate hostess and gave up to him her own apartment in the Hotel—living room, two bedrooms, two baths, entry, kitchen, butler's pantry—as the only appropriate space available. Coming into the Hotel, the vice president was kept by the Secret Service in a "holding room" until all security arrangements were checked; Mrs. Jenkins remembers not being happy with the idea of the Secret Service going through her dresser drawers looking for bombs. The Secret Service also installed a red phone to keep Rockefeller in touch with the White House. The next morning, after Rockefeller had left, the phone briefly was still there, though disconnected, and "I touched it before they came to get it," Janet Jenkins admits. Rockefeller took room service meals, the principal feature of which was a steak prepared by Chef Heinz Schlagel.

Vice President Gerald Ford was a visitor in July 1974, brought to Roanoke on a political mission of some sort. He was put up in the Presidential Suite, a collection of rooms on the third floor. The designation referred not to the Washington presidents but to the Roanoke ones, those working across the street in the railroad's general offices. Its use was not exclusive to those presidents; it was rentable by anyone who fancied the space and was willing to pay the premium price. The suite was furnished, according to Janet Jenkins, not in the cool, airy, colorful style of the rest of the guest rooms but in the overwrought fashion of the late Victorian era, when the Hotel was built. "A lot of fringes and heavy curtains and dark colors and perhaps plush; there was a round settee in the middle of the living room. A man told me he thought it looked like a brothel. I told him I didn't know, but that I would take his word for it."

She recalled Ford as a nice man who "emanated a wonderful warmth and disposition, but just the same the visit was a trying thing—a heavy responsibility."

Warren Webb tended to the needs of Alabama governor George Wallace during a Hotel Roanoke stop in his campaign for the presidential nomination. One of those needs was a large steak dinner he delivered to the governor's room, along with a large fruit basket. The entire thing had to be undone to permit the Secret Service

OPPOSITE Hotel business was not all political carryings-on and conventions and dinners. There were extravagant flower shows as well. *Courtesy of N&W Photo, K.L. Miller Collection.*

to examine it piece by piece. There was also a stethoscope somehow involved in the examination. One Secret Service agent told Webb that the Hotel was "the nicest place we've been in."

Vice President George Bush ate his dinner at a table in the middle of the Regency Room's dance floor with his Secret Service detail at nearby tables, and earlier, roaming around the Hotel lobby, had encountered General Manager Peter Kipp. "Hiya, Peter, how ya doin?"

Private citizen Richard Nixon was in the Hotel in 1966 speaking on Vietnam, and President Richard Nixon was in the Hotel the night before Linwood Holton's election as governor. Walker conducted Nixon to his suite on the latter occasion. For his dinner, he ordered only bouillon and dry toast but insisted that his Secret Service detail get whatever they wanted. "An interesting man," is Walker's judgment. The Republican Party twice nominated Holton for governor in uproarious celebrations, with Ronald Reagan speaking at the 1969 convention, and in November of that year celebrated victory in the Crystal Ballroom. (A visitor to the Hotel on many occasions, Holton is remembered by Warren Webb as an outgoing, friendly man who would often take his meals with the chef and some of the staff at the chef's table in the kitchen.) Presidential candidate Jimmy Carter spoke to his party's faithful in 1976. In 1988, Oliver North, facing hooting demonstrators, drove up to the Hotel with a police escort and went inside to speak at a Marshall Coleman campaign breakfast, where he declared that he would not forget how Coleman had stood up for him in his own troubles.

Even taking into account the eminent figures (political and otherwise) who have gathered at the Hotel, certainly the grandest convocation there—and possibly in the entire Commonwealth—occurred on Virginia Night in December 1967. Governor Mills Godwin and all six of his living predecessors—J. Lindsay Almond, John S. Battle, Colgate W. Darden, Albertis S. Harrison, Thomas B. Stanley and William M. Tuck—and their wives were guests of honor at a banquet and dance in the Crystal Ballroom. Not since the stars were painted on the ceiling of the Oval Room thirty years before had the Hotel seen such a constellation.

The idea of the gathering came from discussions between Carl Thurston, the suave, sophisticated promotion-minded man who succeeded George Denison as general manager in 1964, and Fred Walker, then sales manager and later general manager. (Walker is the only Hotel Roanoke general manager to have attended Oxford University. Stationed in England during the Second World War, he took advantage of a special army program and spent nine months studying in Balliol College and living in the same rooms that in the last quarter of the nineteenth century housed Herbert Asquith, who became prime minister in 1908. Doreen Hamilton Fishwick's distinction is that she is the only Hotel Roanoke general manager to have sung professionally on the operatic stage.)

Virginia Night's invitation list included the heads of the one hundred top corporations in Virginia. With the railroad's logistical cooperation and fueled by the determination to make it a newsworthy as well as a memorable event, Walker traveled aboard a Norfolk and Western Railway office car to New York to fetch Charlotte Curtis, the gifted women's editor of the *New York Times*. It was the first time she had ever ridden on an office car. Joining the group in Washington on the return trip were Herb Blunk, former president of the American Hotel and Motel Association and senior vice president of Hilton Hotels, and Richard Joseph, travel editor of *Esquire* magazine, who had flown to Washington from overseas. The luggage of this sophisticated world traveler, Walker remembers, was tied up with a piece of rope. The next morning, the tireless Walker in the NW aircraft ran a shuttle from Roanoke around the state to pick up most of the guests of honor.

Dinner started with seafood cocktail à la Russe and went on to tomato bouillon with cheese straws, poached filet of turbot with lobster wine sauce, roast tenderloin of beef with stuffed mushrooms à la Virginienne, pesillees potatoes, fiddleheads, hearts of palm salad, cherries jubilee and coffee. There were two wines—Haut Sauternes 1964 and Chateau Lafitte 1961—and liqueurs.

And what are fiddleheads, Ms. Curtis wanted to know. Walker said that they are young fern sprouts, imported, and supposed to taste like beans. Lieutenant Governor Fred Pollard said that "they don't look like anything that grows around here." Ms. Curtis reported to readers of the *Times* that "everybody seemed to like them."

The stars of the show, the governors, were "amiable, well-mannered and venerable," Curtis wrote. "They came from all over their beloved state to this their western frontier to drink, dine and dance at what was ostensibly the 85th anniversary of Hotel Roanoke....They were done up in dinner jackets of various eras, and during the ensuing cocktail reception, when they weren't being cornered by the other guests, they wrapped their arms around one another and talked about old times."

She added that the Reverend Noel C. Taylor, president of the Roanoke Ministers' Conference and pastor of High Street Baptist Church (and later a many-term mayor of Roanoke), delivered the invocation and benediction. "He too represented an old Virginia family; his ancestors were among the first slaves."

In these political events, most of which she observed from her various job assignments, Janet Jenkins preserved a pretty neutrality: "I was a Republican, then I was a Democrat, then I was a Republican again."

(Only three years before, after the passage of the Civil Rights Act, Janet Jenkins had welcomed the first black guest into the Hotel. She was Mahalia Jackson, the

distinguished gospel singer. Doing so was one of Mrs. Jenkins's proudest moments. The singer's agent had called from New York earlier to make the arrangements; on her departure, Ms. Jackson stopped to thank Mrs. Jenkins for her "graciousness and courtesy." The incident "opened the door to a new and finer era in the Hotel's life," Mrs. Jenkins has said.)

Virginia Night with its spectacular menu predated by several years the arrival in 1971 of Executive Chef Heinz Schlagel. Born in West Germany, he started his craft as a fifteen-year-old apprentice and, working in hotels all across Europe, rose from assistant to the cook to cook, sous-chef and finally chef. Eventually, he found his way to Montreal, where he met Ken Wilkey—"an outgoing personality"—and later to the Beverly Hillcrest Hotel in California. There he fed Hollywood luminaries—Dean Martin, William Holden and Anthony Quinn, among others. John Wayne liked a soup, a small serving of meat and a salad; Diahann Carroll liked a raw meat entrée, though a fair observer would have reason to believe that the servings should be the

ABOVE The Hotel in a 1947 snow scene. *Courtesy of N&W Photo, K.L. Miller Collection.*

OPPOSITE A great night for Virginians occurred in December 1967, when the governor and six of his predecessors were in the Hotel to celebrate its eighty-fifth birthday. *Seated, left to right*: Thomas B. Stanley, then governor Mills Godwin, John S. Battle; *standing*: Mr. and Mrs. William M. Tuck, Mr. and Mrs. Albertis S. Harrison, Mr. and Mrs. Colgate W. Darden, Mrs. and Mr. J. Lindsay Almond. *Courtesy of the Historical Society of Western Virginia.*

other way around. When Wilkey was named general manager of Hotel Roanoke, he sent for his former colleague. Schlagel found the Hotel to be much like some hotels in Germany: "old style, comfortable-old."

Schlagel arrived on a Tuesday and immediately had to prepare dinner for the Norfolk and Western Board of Directors on Wednesday. It was a simple matter: consommé au riz, filet de sole marguerite, tournedos rossini, asparagus, a Belgian endive salad, cheese and fruit tray and petit fours with demitasses of Colombian coffee, followed by liqueurs. It lasted two hours. "I think it was a hit," he said later, buoyed by the compliments NW president John Fishwick and other directors extended. These board dinners were highlights of Schlagel's Hotel career, when Fishwick selected the wines and took a hand in planning the menu.

Schlagel's cosmopolitan tastes and continental cuisine brought what one observer has called a "significant improvement" to the Hotel's menu. He added more or less for the first time bouillabaisse, escargot and frog legs. But he also tried a "little bit of everything" in the kitchen and learned to like Smithfield ham and spoonbread. He never said "we can't do that," even when he was preparing something he had never prepared before—like coon and other game that was brought to him for special handling. He oversaw a crew of twenty to thirty people, including a baker, three breakfast cooks and one person who fixed only sandwiches. Schlagel later went on to become chef at Roanoke's Shenandoah Club.

Chapter 5

A DIFFICULT DECISION AND
WHAT FOLLOWED FROM IT

Early in the afternoon of July 26, 1989, Arnold B. McKinnon, chairman of the board and chief executive officer of Norfolk Southern Corporation, sat in Hotel Roanoke's Pine Room, scene of many a revel in the Hotel's long and glittering history. With him, and about to make some history of their own—though without much revelry—were Dr. James McComas, president of Virginia Polytechnic Institute and State University, and Roanoke mayor Noel C. Taylor and their assorted paladins. Then McKinnon stood up and told a room full of journalists and civic leaders that Norfolk Southern Corporation would donate its 107-year-old Hotel Roanoke to Virginia Polytechnic Institute and State University to be turned into a major facility for conferences and continuing education.

A few hundred words further into his statement, McKinnon also announced that Norfolk Southern would build an office building in Roanoke to accommodate in a new and efficient environment its 1,200 officers and office employees. Then spoke Dr. James McComas, the new president of Virginia Polytechnic Institute and State University.

"As a land grant institution, Virginia Tech has a unique mission to serve the needs of the people of Virginia. With this gift, Virginia Tech will establish a management/executive development and continuing education facility within the confines of a renovated and restored Hotel Roanoke. Virginia Tech," he said, "will lead the effort to restore the Hotel and return it to its rightful place as the grand dame of Roanoke's hotels....I thank Arnold McKinnon, John Fishwick and the board of Norfolk Southern Corporation for this important gift to the future of Virginia Tech and to the future of Roanoke."

In local newspaper coverage the next day, the gift of the Hotel took second place behind the office building announcement. Reaction to the latter by some of the city's mandarins, who had hoped the railroad would buy into plans for a new landmark office tower then under development, ranged from resignation through petulance to fury: "It would have been wonderful for the city," mourned one. "It's the railroad's way of telling Roanoke they're out of here; flowers on the grave," bleated another.

All of this, plus unseemly personal animus directed at Fishwick, is, even years after the event, hard to understand. After all, Norfolk Southern was preparing to make a more than $25 million investment in Roanoke's downtown, a demonstration to even the slowest mind that the railroad and its works would remain and prosper in the city, as it had done for more than a century.

This is merely by-the-way. The major reason why the gift of the Hotel didn't show up until the bottom of the second paragraph of the news story was simply that by then, it wasn't much of a surprise, as surprises go. Two weeks before the announcement, it was reported that Virginia Tech's Board of Visitors had authorized the administration to "submit a formal proposal to Norfolk Southern regarding the Hotel Roanoke." Roanoke city officials were quoted as being "extremely excited about the role Tech might play in plans for the conference center" and the conversion of Hotel Roanoke

ABOVE A Hotel publicity photograph from the early 1960s sought to emphasize the Hotel as a family place to stay. *Courtesy of Special Collections, University Libraries, Virginia Tech.*

to a conference hotel, a project that in one form or another had been on the city's plate for a long time. And now it was approaching reality.

Playing his cards close, Fishwick told a reporter simply, "I know the Hotel is a problem in the long run; that's all I can say."

Then, on the day before McKinnon's press conference, there appeared a long and largely accurate story reporting what was about to occur. It was headlined "NS to Give Tech Hotel" and quoted Fishwick: "I think it's the greatest thing to hit Roanoke in my lifetime. We're going to change this town from a blue-collar town into a university town." Minnis Ridenour, executive vice president of Virginia Tech and its chief business officer, agreed: "We're betting on the long term impact of Virginia Tech and the impact it will have on Roanoke."

So when McKinnon stood up to face the cameras and notebooks, most people knew what he was going to say about the Hotel. What they didn't know was what had brought Norfolk Southern to such a portentous step involving a hallowed Roanoke symbol.

As it happened, several events and conditions in Norfolk Southern and its hotel subsidiary became congruent in late 1980s. For one, Norfolk Southern's Annual Report for 1987 reported in austere prose (but not austere enough to exclude a pardonable note of pride) that Hotel Roanoke was "a real estate activity that contributed positive earnings....A restoration program begun in 1986, coupled with new marketing initiatives, returned the hotel operation to positive earnings for the first time in many years." Not a large sum, to be sure, but sufficient to allow the Hotel's proprietors to put away the red ink that had so lavishly and customarily ornamented the books since 1980. Further, "Capital expenditures of more than $1 million in 1987 and 1988 are being funded wholly from the hotel's internally generated cash flow." These expenditures involved principally remodeling and redecorating its guest rooms, one floor at a time. (This work continued virtually up to the Hotel's closing. Later, when asked about these expenditures at a time when no return on the investment was possible, McKinnon declared simply, "As long as we had guests, we were determined to maintain quality.")

At the same time, such earnings as the Hotel was generating were clearly inadequate to finance the major—$32 to $35 million capital expenditures needed mainly for a new heating and cooling system (principal source for some while of guest complaints), although there were other pressing requirements as well. Such a major program would be necessary to enhance quality and competitive standards, "to make it first class" in the words of Arnold McKinnon. Whatever happened, he added, "we recognized the need to handle the Hotel in a manner consistent with our citizenship in the Valley."

Was an investment of that magnitude by Norfolk Southern likely? Apparently not very. Norfolk Southern's future, McKinnon has said, suggested that the capital resources the Hotel would need might well be put to better use elsewhere. "Elsewhere" most certainly included a new General Office Building in Roanoke. The existing two office buildings—one built before the turn of the century, the other in 1931—were, like the Hotel across the street, old, increasingly inefficient, underpopulated and costly to maintain. (The elevators in the older of the two were temperamental and given to whimsical and sometimes prolonged stops between floors. One employee said he tried to be sure whenever he entered the car that he had 1) been to the bathroom, 2) had with him something to read or eat, and preferably both.) McKinnon told the press conference that the "largest buildings were in need of repair and rehabilitation if we are to continue them in service.... Our studies indicated that it would be more efficient and economic to consolidate the majority of our Roanoke personnel in a new building."

In October 1985, Fishwick, though he had retired as Norfolk and Western Railway's chairman and was at the time associated with a Washington law firm, had been prevailed upon by Norfolk Southern's then chairman, Robert B. Claytor, to return to Roanoke and oversee the Hotel's operations and to determine what, if anything might be done with it. He moved back into the penthouse where he and his family had lived for many years, just across the street from his railroad office. (A perhaps apocryphal story has it that during one of the country's perennial energy crises in the 1970s, a reporter asked Fishwick what he was doing to promote energy conservation. "I walk to work," he is supposed to have replied.)

From that aerie, he watched over the property and absorbed its problems. His task was, he told a reporter at the time, a "sort of labor of love. I don't know if anything can be done." In truth, the prospect he faced then was formidable: Hotel Roanoke had been losing money and would—except for 1987—continue this dismal course. The losses sometimes approached $1 million a year. It was in debt to its owner, and it faced major competition from local motels, which, though lacking Hotel Roanoke's charm and tradition, nevertheless could offer its patrons state-of-the-art facilities beyond the Grand Old Lady's capabilities.

One thing he did was to hire a new general manager, Doreen Hamilton, a brisk, no-nonsense professional hotelier from Philadelphia's Barclay Hotel, where she had been managing director. Her credentials included managerial experience at New York's American Stanhope and Barclay Hotels, and her forte was cost-cutting and tight and accurate budgeting. She later said that she had to ask "Where is it?" when she was told about the job opening in Roanoke and she had not even heard of its eponymous Hotel. The workforce she was to manage was still shaken from a six-month-long strike that had aroused deep and divisive feelings in the community, but she was quick to put those matters in the past. She took charge and, as one former subordinate said, "got involved."

After a careful exploration of the books, she concluded that the Hotel could not be made financially stable in the presence of its large debts to the parent Norfolk Southern Corporation. With the understanding that the debt would be forgiven, she accepted the job. She had also discovered, as her former staff assistant Vickie Stump Cutting so succinctly put it, that "some Roanokers didn't pay their bills."

The books revealed significant outstanding debts run up and unpaid-for meals, parties, meetings and so on. Mrs. Hamilton had not been on the job very long when she began to pursue with considerable vigor the payment of these obligations. It was a situation, Mrs. Hamilton felt strongly, that could not be tolerated any further, and after a few hortatory telephone calls and a few clearly expressed letters, she was gratified to see that indeed, it was not.

While all this was happening in the Norfolk Southern/Hotel Roanoke orbit, the city manager, looking at the possibility of a major conference/trade center to be associated with Hotel Roanoke, had formed a Trade Center Task Force in 1985 and undertaken a study by the public accounting firm of Laventhol & Horwath to determine the center's feasibility. This would be part of Roanoke's long-term development plan. The study's conclusion was yes, it was feasible, but only if a modern three-hundred- to four-hundred-room convention hotel was in support of it. Earlier, Norfolk Southern and Dominion Bankshares (now First Union Bank), perhaps the entire region's principal banking institution, had collaborated on another study, this one by the RTKL firm, to look at the project from a different viewpoint: whether the trade center could support either a modernized Hotel Roanoke or a new convention-type hotel. The answer was affirmative. But "modern" was the operative word in both studies, which would seem to eliminate Hotel Roanoke as it then stood.

The person of David Caudill now assumes a major role in the labyrinthine events that ultimately led to the July 26 announcement. He was vice chairman of Dominion Bankshares, an alumnus of Virginia Tech and chairman of the city's Trade Center Task Force. Indefatigable in his search for ways to make a trade center—or conference center or exhibit hall (concepts for all three circulated freely as the participants worked toward a useful focus)—a viable reality for Roanoke, Caudill held frequent conversations with City Manager Robert Herbert and the city's economic development director, Brian Wishneff.

The three met frequently in Caudill's office, a place to "talk 'what-ifs' as a sort of debating society," Herbert later said. In meeting after meeting, "we just let matters develop. The loss of the Hotel would mean a major loss of business to the city; we all knew we didn't want that. At the same time, studies showed a need to maximize revenues from the Civic Center. An Exhibit Hall—or whatever it would be called—would need a base-load permanent tenant to provide perhaps 25 percent occupancy

to make it viable. We talked of establishing a mart of some sort, a continuing event in the city—a medical mart, a rug mart, even. From there, it was a quick step in our 'what-if' sessions from rugs to an 'education mart,' and that meant Virginia Tech."

But what interest would Virginia Tech have in acquiring a hotel at all, much less one in Roanoke? Caudill knew how to find out.

It was about this time that Virginia Tech had found a new president, Dr. James McComas, president of the University of Toledo. He had not yet left the one for the other. Warner Dalhouse, Caudill's chief at Dominion, was eager to add McComas to his board of directors. He thought he and Caudill ought to take the bank's aircraft to Toledo and make the offer, and Caudill, Herbert and Wishneff saw the trip as a chance to explore the new president's interest in the hotel/conference center issue. Four people went on the bank's aircraft to Toledo: the two bankers, Roanoke mayor Reverend Noel C. Taylor and Herbert. Dr. McComas was about to have earnest visitors.

Herbert, in his approach, reminded McComas of Virginia Tech's mission as a land grant university—the commonwealth as a campus, continuing education and outreach. McComas had no need of the sales pitch. His own University of Toledo had earlier become involved in a similar role with the city and an existing hotel. He was able to show the Roanokers a large computer-filled classroom where the university was

ABOVE Typical lobby scene, probably in the late 1940s or early '50s. *Courtesy of N&W Photo, K.L. Miller Collection.*

conducting retraining education for employees displaced by an industrial shutdown—the idea at work. The visitors lunched with the McComases at their home. Not just the lunch but the visit was, in Herbert's words, "a love feast."

Thus, when McComas soon took up his station in Blacksburg, the university was prepared to move ahead. Tech's plenipotentiary was Minnis Ridenour, executive vice president and chief business officer, who soon joined the Herbert-Caudill discussion group. Ridenour, expanding on the "education mart" concept, began seeing the hotel/conference center as an industry, an entity with profit and growth in mind, a position in no way incompatible with the Tech view of outreach and continuing education. The conventional wisdom held that the Hotel couldn't stand alone, but with a conference center...?

Thinking on more or less parallel lines was Norfolk Southern's man-in-the-hotel, Fishwick. Though primarily representing Norfolk Southern's interest, he shared with the others a desire to find a way to bring to reality a major meeting facility, settle the Hotel dilemma and at the same time promote Tech's own goals.

Into this came the tireless Caudill, shuttling back and forth among the city, Virginia Tech and Norfolk Southern, like a Blue Ridge Metternich, carrying from one to the other sometimes oblique, sometimes vague ideas, scenarios, positions.

Finally, Fishwick, on his own and in his words, "without any backing or authorization from Norfolk [corporate headquarters], flat out" asked Caudill if Virginia Tech would consider accepting the Hotel as a gift. The question was welcome, because Tech had already come to the conclusion that it would. For Norfolk Southern, McKinnon approved this direct approach, seeing it, as he later told an interviewer, as a way "to demonstrate our commitment to the city of Roanoke by keeping Hotel Roanoke as a functioning entity, and to open a new level of cooperation with Tech and its continuing education and outreach programs." (Norfolk Southern's board of directors by action at its July 25, 1989 meeting made the donation of the Hotel to Virginia Tech official.) The city for its part agreed to supply an amount that eventually rose to $12.8 million for the conference center, which not only guaranteed a revived and operating Hotel Roanoke but also fulfilled its own original dream.

There was an all-star cast of players in this bravura performance, and it is one of the more rewarding reflections on the whole business that each of the principals was eager to extend large chunks of credit for its success to others. Fishwick said that "McComas had the courage and vision to see all of the disparate elements in this project, and grasp instinctively how it would benefit the community, the Hotel, and mostly his notion of what he wanted his University to be in the future." Ridenour and Herbert credit Caudill; Caudill credits Fishwick and Herbert. In turn, Herbert had special praise for the late Horace Fralin, who, though suffering from terminal illness, devoted time and expended irreplaceable energy to work on the project. Virginia Tech, said McKinnon, played a "serendipitous role, providing continuity and commitment to Roanoke and a unique opportunity to the school."

All of the converging tides, the disparate personalities and their egos, the elation, sorrow and promise met in the Pine Room on that summer day to mark a sad end and a brave beginning for Hotel Roanoke. For its employees, however, there was only the sad end.

Hamilton had earlier that day informed her senior managers of the forthcoming decision, and they, in turn, informed their own staffs, supplemented by memos posted in employee work areas.

"We were shocked" at the melancholy news, according to Vickie Stump Cutting, administrative assistant to the general manager. "We didn't know what to say. A lot of us had thought that something had to happen—perhaps a chain taking over." Hotel employees, like everyone else in the Roanoke Valley, had read press reports about the donation of the Hotel to Virginia Tech and earlier rumors about its sale. Alex Alexander and Billy Davis, however, were not especially shocked at the news; "we had heard the rumors—who hadn't?—and besides," said Billy later, smiling, "we were in a position to hear things."

Donation of the Hotel was one thing, but shutting it down was quite another, especially to employees, some of whom represented the third or even fourth generation of their families who had worked there, raised and educated their children there and been a proud and living part of the Roanoke tradition. Not even the trauma of a six-month-long strike and the sometimes painful divisions and hard feelings that followed its settlement could dislocate the comradeship nurtured by the bad news.

"We were all in the same predicament," said Bruce Coffey, front desk manager at the time, in a later interview. "We consoled one another, encouraged one another. And above all, we kept the Hotel operating at its usual high standards. Whatever happened, we weren't going to change that. We still had our pride." (Years after the closing, many employees still kept in touch with each other. Billy Davis, Alex Alexander and Mike Mason lunch together regularly to relive their life-careers; Vickie Cutting, Bruce Coffey, former controller Lynne Schumacher and former engineer Mark Lambert in their own gatherings, among other things, talked Schumacher through her CPA study and listened to Lambert's reports on the renovation work on the Hotel, where he worked for the contractor after the closing.)

Chapter 6

SETTING OUT THE DECK CHAIRS

In this climate—made up in equal parts of determination, sorrow, uncertainty and pride—Doreen Hamilton, now Mrs. John P. Fishwick, had to continue to operate the Hotel and simultaneously prepare to shut it down on November 30. There were arrangements to be made to dispose of the furnishings and cancel reservations and meetings scheduled after the closing date. Ranking in equal importance with all of these and other pressing matters was the question of any financial settlement with employees.

Although under the existing contract with Local 32 of the Hotel and Restaurant Union the Hotel was not required to make any severance payments to its unionized employees, Mrs. Fishwick took it as a matter of right that there should be a settlement "fair and honorable," in her words, and she so informed the Hotel's corporate masters in Norfolk headquarters. Concern for the well-being of employees and recognition of their importance to the success and reputation of the Hotel had always been a guiding principle in her management style. Indeed, at one point in her general managership she had wanted to provide a raise to all of the Hotel's employees, even though the union had not made such a request. Legally, however, this was impossible, for the curious reason that without union negotiations, the action would have been considered an unfair labor practice.

Calling local reporters to a press conference on August 31, the general manager told them:

> *We have some good news to share with you....As you are well aware both management and the employees have considered ourselves to be a family and I am delighted to report*

to you today that through the efforts of the Hotel and the union headed by Mr. Minor Christian, we have reached a severance agreement which, as far as we know, is better than any severance offered hotel employees in the United States....

Ever since...the announcement was made regarding the Hotel's closing, the Hotel's desire has been to lessen the burden which this closing may place on employees. We feel that this agreement will now allow the employees to take the time necessary to seek other employment or, in some cases, even to change their career paths.

I have...assurances that our employees intend to see that the service offered at the Hotel Roanoke will continue to be of the highest quality right up until the last dinner is served and the last drink order is taken on the night of November 30.

Then, ever the consummate marketer, she added, "I trust that everyone will take the opportunity to visit this grand old lady at least one more time to sample the ambiance and the service which have been the very backbone of the Hotel Roanoke for the past 107 years and before she receives her new look for the 21st Century."

The agreement's terms were simple. Every person employed at the Hotel before July 26, 1989 (the day the closing was announced), would receive a week's pay at the employee's current wage rate for each year of employment. For full-time employees, the severance was based on a forty-hour week, for part-time employees on a twenty-four-hour week. Minimum payments of $500 and $300, respectively, were established. Those laid off because of lack of work would be eligible as well. Further, all employees would receive a letter of reference specifying that employment was terminated because of the Hotel's closing.

That matter settled, Mrs. Fishwick moved on to another. She had determined that the Hotel's passage from the railroad's ownership would best be marked with a spectacular, invitation-only Closing Banquet in the chandeliered Crystal Ballroom. She envisioned it as an event so dignified and steeped in traditional Hotel Roanoke graciousness that the community would say of the Hotel with mournful pride, as Malcolm said of Cawdor, that nothing in its life became it like the leaving it.

The Closing Banquet was held on November 28, 1989, and attendance was limited by space to about six hundred invited persons, the standard seating capacity for a dinner to be followed by dancing. The event became what is known as a "hot ticket," prized by those who had one, coveted by those who didn't. Bruce Coffey fielded dozens of telephone calls from people who wanted to buy tickets. Because the dinner dance was essentially a local celebration of a local institution by local people, its guest list showed the Roanoke Valley's political and business magnificoes, movers and shakers and a handful of Norfolk Southern's top echelon from Norfolk. Robert B. Claytor, Roanoke-born, former president of the Norfolk and Western Railway and at the time of the closing the retired chairman of Norfolk Southern, said it was "a bittersweet occasion." He recalled attending debutante balls in the Hotel in the late 1930s as a stag "because I wasn't popular enough to be a date." Another Roanoker in the railroad party coming from Norfolk was John Turbyfill, then executive vice president of finance. He had a more agreeable recollection from his high school days: a rented tuxedo and the prettiest girl in school for a date. Also present at the Closing Banquet with his wife was Linwood Holton, former governor and a former Roanoker whose emotional connection to the city and Hotel operated at several levels. For the general public, thirty invitations were made available to those whose names were drawn at random from a fish bowl placed in the Regency Room.

A Hotel Roanoke waiter. *Courtesy of Norfolk Southern Corporation.*

Sitting down at tables for eight lining three sides of the ballroom, women in fashionable-length dresses and men in black tie found at their places a handsomely designed and printed souvenir booklet. With the booklet and the arsenal of cutlery at each plate was a box containing a large brandy snifter emblazoned with the Hotel Roanoke seal, a gift that for many recipients would never be used but put aside in a place of honor.

Titled *The Grand Old Lady on the Hill*, the booklet's text, charting a course somewhere between soaring paean and melancholy epitaph, read:

> Hotel Roanoke opened Christmas Day, 1882, and closes the week after Thanksgiving, 1989, an embodiment of hospitality and service and elegance for more than a century. It was built in "pretty fields of wheat and corn" by the Norfolk and Western Railroad,

one corner of a quadrilateral with a passenger station, a General Office Building and hammering, steamy railroad shops. Hotel Roanoke passes now to a new life. It is our hope—the management and the staff's—that this booklet will serve not only as reminder of this bittersweet evening but to keep alive memories of honeymoons and dances, Fountain Room dates, political conventions, rehearsal dinners and wedding receptions, after-five aperitifs and a lazy sunning by the pool. Hotel Roanoke has been "our" Hotel to generations of Roanokers. In their name and on your behalf, we pause this evening and offer a toast to our Grand Old Lady on the Hill.

And thank you, Roanoke, for having been here.

The impeccable Hotel Roanoke service was, for this last gallant show, burnished to an even brighter perfection. As the Bruce Swartz Quintet played, a regiment of servers brought in dinner, anchored by the Hotel's two traditional culinary triumphs. The menu, printed in the booklet, consisted of peanut soup, sliced tenderloin of beef with fresh asparagus, glazed carrots and Duchess potato, spoonbread and, for dessert, twin mousse and raspberry puree, with tea or coffee. There were two Virginia wines.

After dinner, Doreen Fishwick proposed a toast to the Hotel's past and its almost mystical union with the community that virtually grew under its gaze: "To her glorious past—may she sleep well, and may she awaken with all the charm of today to face a bright and prosperous 21st Century." And then, in a moment that brought tears to most, all sang a chorus of "Auld Lang Syne." It was at this moment, one man said, that the finality of what was happening came to him. "Up to then," he said, "it had been an abstract possibility, almost theoretical. Now, we all knew that we would never dance under these chandeliers again. It was sad." To join the singing, Fishwick invited all of the dining service staff into the ballroom, to the cheers and applause of the diners. In an emotional scene, guests and serving personnel hugged one another with sobs and tears. For Robert Garland, "it was probably the most elegant banquet ever held in the Crystal Ballroom…a truly memorable and magnificent occasion."

The dancing that followed until eleven o'clock was for many a poignant exercise and for one conjured up a comparison with a grimmer event. "It was like setting out deck chairs on the *Titanic*," he said.

If the Hotel was metaphorically setting out deck chairs, they were not being placed for passengers' comfort but for sale. Agents of the National Content Liquidators, hired by the Hotel to dispose by sale of its entire contents, had been working for nearly a week appraising and tagging the contents for sale, from coffee spoons to laundry equipment, beds to bath towels, televisions to teacups. The sale was to begin at nine o'clock on Monday morning, December 4, three days after the close. Even on the

Dancing for the last time in the Regency Room. *Courtesy of the Historical Society of Western Virginia.*

Hotel's last day, NCL people were careful not to intrude on the sadness of the occasion as they prepared for the huge task awaiting them.

The last night for guests to stay in the Hotel was November 29, and about one hundred of the rooms were taken. Those guests and scores of Roanokers spent part of November 30 prowling the still halls, lobby-sitting, strolling across the graceful Oval Room—always one of the city's loveliest public spaces—and reliving memories in the Crystal Ballroom. Staff continued their work briskly, attending to checkouts, serving lunch and other chores associated with both routine and closing. Charlotte Facella, sales director, had finished the painful task of notifying future conventions—some four or five years away—that their bookings could not be honored.

The big front door had its first and only lock installed. The Regency Room had no reservations left for the last night's dinner serving, and its intimate private space, the Virginia Room, was reserved by Robert Garland for a dinner with family and friends. (Gripped like several others by the recurring motif of the time and its mood of elegant fate, Garland noted that "like the band on the sinking *Titanic*, the music was still playing as we departed the dining room on that last night.") As the late autumn afternoon cooled and darkened, outside preparations moved ahead for the final flag-lowering, Taps-sounding, tear-shedding closing ceremonies around the Reflecting Pool.

Facing the three flagpoles and scores of old friends of the Hotel—at least two from as far away as California—flanked by the Noel C. Taylor Community Choir, a color guard, a congressman, a state senator and a mayor, and watched from the windows of the Norfolk Southern offices across the street, Doreen Fishwick had one more sad speech to give. Sketching the old Hotel's century of history and citing its many firsts, she added:

> *But now, with only seven hours left, we have gathered to say thank you and farewell. Thank you to this community, for 107 years ago you welcomed this Hotel into the life and mainstream of the Valley…to the Norfolk and Western Railway for having had the foresight to build a piece of history…and to the Norfolk Southern Corporation for their generous gift which will make the foundation upon which will be built a major presence of Virginia Tech…and…which will brighten the future and change the character of the Roanoke Valley.*
>
> *To the staff I say thank you for a job well done. You rose to the challenge, difficult as it was, and have kept the Hotel great to the last. To the people of this community, I say thank you for your support over the years.*

When she said, "There will never be another Hotel Roanoke quite like this one," a man standing nearby was heard to mutter in a soft, Virginia-bred voice, "No, ma'am." Ending, she declared, "We who have worked here thank this grand old lady for affording us the privilege of being a part of her 107 years of service."

Reverend Noel C. Taylor, the city's first black mayor—the same Noel C. Taylor mentioned by Charlotte Curtis in her *New York Times* account of the Hotel's Virginia Night in 1967—delivered the sort of eloquent and moving remarks that always characterized his public speech. "The Hotel Roanoke," he said, "has become a symbol to us all. Our citizens cherish its beauty and hold dear the memories of good times. But as we close its doors, lower the flags and sing the final notes, we also open the door to the future of our city."

With appropriate ritual and the sounding of the ghostly, evocative, simple notes of "Taps," the national, state and city flags were lowered and received by Congressman James Olin, State Senator Granger MacFarlane and Mayor Taylor on behalf of the Roanoke Valley History Museum. In the gloom, the shivering crowd, Hotel employees on the porch outside the Regency Room, the choir, the Fishwicks and perhaps even the watchers at the railroad's office windows sang "Auld Lang Syne." There could not have been many dry eyes.

Among the employees was Mike Mason, the bell captain, standing where he had stood for so many years, at the front door waiting for guests. He had worked at the Hotel during school summer vacations and had joined the staff permanently in 1946. Like his colleagues, he felt sadness at the closing, but he was philosophical, even stoic: "It's not the end of the world," he said.

What he had seen in the years immediately preceding the fateful 1989 was worlds apart from what he called "the heydays" of the 1940s, '50s and early '60s. "The hotel was a hustle and bustle," he told Rebecca Burcher, writing for Norfolk Southern's employee publication, *NS World.* "We had business each and every day. From 4 p.m., we had lines. People were coming back and forth. Salesmen would be coming in off the road, and we were very busy every night, up till about 7 or 8 o'clock....In the heydays, it was a family situation. Everybody worked together. Everybody would speak when they saw you, and everybody would joke with you. And then everybody would go and do their work and do it well. It was a family." But now it was time for the family to leave home, and Mike Mason, before he too departed, went to do his work and do it well.

Invited into the Hotel this one last time for warm cider and cookies by the soon-to-be former general manager, and passing through the doors Mike Mason opened for them with his accustomed flourishes and smile, the hundreds who had stood in sadness outside brightened now in the lobby and Oval Room and exchanged reminiscences.

Then after a while, they all went home, and the door was locked behind them.

Chapter 7

TAKING HOME A PIECE
OF THE PAST

The final act opened with the appearance onstage of National Content Liquidators of Dayton, Ohio. It was then a ninety-nine-year-old business that had grown and prospered from selling off the contents of hotels and other such institutions. NCL's offices in Dayton over the years had been furnished with antiques the company had bought for its own account, from chandeliers to paneling, and its walls were covered with prints, art and other memorabilia. Its collection was soon to be enhanced with items from Hotel Roanoke. Frank Long, NCL vice president, characterized Hotel Roanoke as "a pretty neat building" and "one of the more interesting" of the company's six hundred contracts (another of which was the famed Dunes Hotel in Las Vegas, an unlikely yoke-fellow for Roanoke's "modern version of an old English inn").

For the privilege of selling large chunks of Roanoke's history, NCL had paid the hotel an undisclosed amount for the goods it would liquidate. The rumored figure at the time was a quarter of a million dollars, subsequently characterized by Long as "close to accurate." What NCL itself earned from the liquidation was and remained proprietary information. It was to be an "everything goes" sale, continuing as long as there was anything left to sell, which in the event was seventeen days. The sale was vast in scale ("tens of thousands of pieces") and in area (all guest floors, kitchens, laundry, Regency Room, Oval Room, Pine Room and the rest). Before it took place, however, a few exclusions were arranged. The large portraits of George Washington and Robert E. Lee were given to the Roanoke Valley History Museum, railroad memorabilia from the Whistle Stop was reserved for Norfolk Southern, food in the kitchen was given to Roanoke's TAP antipoverty organization and unopened liquor was, under a special arrangement, sold back to the Virginia Alcohol Beverage Control Board store. The handsome paneling in the lobby, chandeliers in the public rooms and ceiling fixtures in the guest rooms were declared exempt, reserved for the renascent Hotel Roanoke to come. Everything else was available and tagged and ready when the doors opened at nine o'clock on the morning of December 4.

For days before the sale was to begin, NCL people had gone through the building, identifying, pricing and tagging everything, taking care not to intrude on staff still occupied with running the Hotel. After November 30, when the last guest had departed and the door was locked, NCL assembled much of the sale merchandise in various places. For example, the Crystal Ballroom was stacked with silverware, china, glass and linens. Tables and chairs from the Regency Room were in the Shenandoah Room. Also in the Shenandoah Room, more than four hundred television sets were arranged, priced upward from $129. Guest room furnishings were kept in place. (During inventory, the NCL had discovered in a large upper-floor closet an apparently forgotten cache of prints and a clock that was thought to have adorned the lobby. Long thought that "they had been up there forty or fifty years." The prints went into the general sale; the clock went to Dayton, where experts put its age at two hundred years.)

NCL's press release in announcing the sale had noted, "Private individuals can furnish their homes elegantly from our fine guest room suites. Hotel and apartment owners can furnish their units from our guest rooms." Also, "business and private individuals will be interested in the large quantities of office furnishings and equipment," and "there are thousands of miscellaneous items such as the Steinway piano, all of the patio and pool side furniture, [and] all lobby furnishings." The NCL people on the job pointed out that unlike other hotels, which typically dispose of their furniture every five years or so, Hotel Roanoke traditionally refinished its chairs, tables, desks and chests, some thought to be almost as old as the building itself. "They were good pieces to begin with, and they have the further advantage of age," which made them highly desirable, according to Long.

Although there were a significant number of commercial buyers on the extensive premises, by far the large majority of those who flocked through the Hotel for the sale were Roanoke Valley individuals who simply wanted something with a demonstrable Hotel Roanoke provenance for themselves, friends, family or institutions, items for use as a continuing tie to the old place.

When the Hotel's door was reopened at nine o'clock on the Monday morning following the closing, December 4, there was already waiting in the cold winter wind a line of people stretching all the way around the building. Standing at the head of the line since 6:15 a.m. and by now uncomfortably cold were Betty Carr Muse and Anne Hammersley, joined shortly by Mona Black, George Cartledge Sr. and Charles Lunsford, representing Center in the Square, home to several of Roanoke's major cultural institutions. Enduring a couple hours' worth of cold, they were there to buy table settings for seventy-two to use for the center's receptions, luncheons or dinners in the area known as the Cartledge Connection, named for a major financial supporter and patron of the center, who at that moment stood and shivered like everyone else in the long line.

The party had planned the buying spree carefully, having assigned specific duties to each so that no time would be wasted when they stepped into the sale's whirlwind to gather up the pieces. In the Crystal Ballroom, where sales, in Long's words, "went like firecrackers," they found, oddly, only forty-eight cups and saucers and no water goblets at all with the HR logo, a shortage possibly explained by imputing pilferage to the Hotel's guests in the closing weeks. The center's new dinner plates, salad plates, bread and butter plates (seven to nine dollars each), what cups and saucers (five dollars each) were available and assorted knives, forks and spoons were put in ever-growing stacks in one corner of the ballroom.

Protecting the heap from inquisitive eyes and grasping hands, Mona Black and Anne Hammersley covered it with their coats. Stationed there, Lunsford "stood like a sentinel" to fend off the ravening hordes roaming the Hotel. Cartledge had earlier arranged for cartons to be brought from his furniture establishment, and into these went the table settings, wrapped in tablecloths and napkins, bought from stock as well. The boxes, a coffee urn and nine round tables from the Regency Room and eight matching chairs for each were delivered by his trucks to the center.

With "people running around and grabbing, the whole business was a combat mission" for Mona Black; and, in fact, in the course of picking out and holding onto these last pieces, a hand-to-hand combat indeed nearly did develop. Another buyer had decided that he would take two tables from those she had with some difficulty collected herself. "No," she declared firmly after a brief confrontation with the usurper. "That is unacceptable. These are my tables. Look for your own somewhere else."

The Hotel's events board, still showing the name of Ray Ebbett, the lobby pianist, was marked $165 and bought for the Roanoke Valley History Museum by its director, Dr. Nancy Connelly. The lobby bar went for $1,925 to a local Roanoke couple for their home. The planters that divided the bar from the lobby proper were bought by a Roanoke restaurant, which also acquired additional Hotel Roanoke flavor with the large table from the Oval Room, a number of mirrors and chairs from guest rooms and several pieces of kitchen equipment. An Atlanta firm bought the heavy-duty laundry equipment. The portrait of Kylene Barker, Miss Virginia/America, which had hung on the wall at the head of Peacock Alley, was priced—and bought—for $225. Long himself bought two dozen brandy glasses, and a partner at NCL bought the Steinway for his home.

Buyers lined up every one of the seventeen days "as if they were waiting for a seat on a roller coaster," said Long. Inside at any one time, there were typically 1,500 to 2,000 potential buyers, and people were admitted in groups of 25 or so to replace those departing. Cashiers were set up in the major areas to take cash and credit cards, but no checks.

The Center in the Square people got everything they wanted. Their excursion, though sometimes fraught, was successful, as were uncountable others who came out of the Hotel laden with chairs, desks, framed prints, Venetian blinds, champagne holders, waste baskets and other impedimenta. It was a clearly a success for NCL and ultimately, in some ways, for Hotel Roanoke itself. A success and satisfaction for many, but not everyone saw the sale in those congenial terms.

Robert Garland, who observed the life and times of the Hotel and its people with an almost Pepysian eye, was among those who went into the Hotel for the sale. Perhaps he witnessed the same sort of "running and grabbing" Black observed. The whole event resembled for him "a band of gypsies swarming down on their prey like killer bees. I could not watch as they disassembled and undressed her. I left empty-handed save for the memories. As I walked back to my car, I thought to myself that the Hotel had become a victim of the changing times. It had succumbed to the chrome and plastic crowd and the bottom line impresarios with their computers and their Teflon kitchens." Michael Ramsey was similarly affected. With a background in the Roanoke Chamber of Commerce and the Convention Bureau, he had nurtured a close and affectionate connection with the Hotel and its staff and thought it was "a rather tawdry garage sale leaving nothing to symbolically tie the new hotel with the one it will replace."

A few days before Christmas, the sale came to end. Fishwick and a small staff moved across the street to office space in the Norfolk and Western's executive suite to deal with final financial matters. In the Hotel, the lights were turned off, except for the few needed for security; the heat was turned off, except for what was needed to prevent mold and damp; the staff departed, except for the few needed to patrol the empty corridors. Everything that had given life and warmth and flavor and style to the life of Hotel Roanoke was gone, and it was left alone, silent and dark.

Silent, yes, and dark. But was it dead?

No, it was not. For like King Arthur, Hotel Roanoke fell asleep in its own Avalon, waiting for its time to come again. And come again it did, old memories preserved undimmed and brought to light once more.

Chapter 8

HOTEL REVIVUS

At a rally in Roanoke's Civic Center on January 11, 1993, an event timed to allow live coverage for the six o'clock news by three television stations, Thomas Robertson announced that Renew Roanoke had raised $5 million for Hotel Roanoke and thereby assured its reopening. (Not long after, Norfolk Southern contributed another $2 million, an amount thirty times what the railroad paid for the original Hotel.) It was the final and long-awaited piece in the financial package.

Robertson, Reverend Noel C. Taylor and David Bowers, Taylor's successor as mayor, had chaired the Renew Roanoke campaign. It lasted only seven weeks and involved three hundred volunteers and three thousand contributors from all over the country, but mostly from the Roanoke Valley, all moved by fond memories of the place.

Renew Roanoke was born in a sense of urgency. Virginia Tech had set a deadline of December 31, 1992, for the financing of the reopening of the Hotel. By late fall, there remained a major dollar gap. The entire community took up the challenge and in an unprecedented fundraiser over the Christmas holidays succeeded. Its success was more than sentiment; it was also, as Robertson said later, sound economics. For its millions, Roanoke not only preserved and enhanced Hotel Roanoke but also became a one-third owner with the Virginia Tech Foundation.

The way was clear. Hotel Roanoke would live.

The successful Renew Roanoke effort represented the final piece of a complex financial strategy to position the Hotel Roanoke to not just survive but prosper. The Virginia Tech Foundation, Inc. discovered early on that financing a hotel during the economic downturn of the early 1990s was difficult. The distress and closings of many hotels nationwide suggested that a conventional loan for the renovation of Hotel Roanoke was unlikely.

With this in mind, the Virginia Tech Foundation recruited a group of Roanoke Valley civic and business leaders to assist in constructing a financing and development package for the project. Members of the ad hoc group were well known. They included the late Horace Fralin, president of the foundation and of his own company, Fralin and Waldron, Inc.; Tom Robertson, president, Carilion Health System and co-chair of Renew Roanoke; David Caudill, vice chairman, First Union (Dominion) Bank; John Rocovich, Moss and Rocovich, P.C.; George Cartledge Jr., president, Grand Piano and Furniture Co.; James Harvey, member, Roanoke City Council; Joseph Stephenson, president, Shenandoah Life Insurance Co.; Bob Herbert, Roanoke city manager; and Minnis Ridenour, executive vice president, and Raymond Smoot, vice president for finance and treasurer, both of Virginia Tech.

In the face of difficulties and the demands of individual job responsibilities, this public-spirited group, working with six financing institutions, the U.S. Department of Housing and Urban Development, the City of Roanoke, the Virginia Tech Foundation and Hotel Roanoke's new operating company, Doubletree Hotels Corporation, and including the Renew Roanoke campaign, produced a $27.5 million package. This guaranteed that Hotel Roanoke would reopen.

The broader story of financing, construction and reopening the Hotel had its share of disappointments, perseverance and triumph and deserves to be told.

The Hotel Roanoke and Conference Center formally reopened on April 29, 1995. A grand ribbon-cutting and dedication ceremony featured Virginia Governor George Allen, who trumpeted the landmark's renewed presence in the region: "It is a signal of confidence in the region's future. It has a far greater significance for the region and state."

The reopening marked the successful culmination of yeoman efforts by civic, education, business and philanthropic leaders throughout the Roanoke and New River Valleys. Accompanying the cadre of politicians all seeking to bask in the success were fourth and fifth graders from Roanoke's Monterey Elementary School, who sang an original composition scored just for the ceremony titled "The Grand Old Lady." The musical celebration included Daniel Womack, a blind ninety-year-old gospel singer and former employee of the hotel, and the Virginia Tech Quantum Brass.

Roanoke Mayor David Bowers invoked President Abraham Lincoln's words in describing the moment: "Few people will note or long remember what we said here today, but Roanoke will never forget what we did."

OPPOSITE Demolition and construction before the hotel reopening in 1995. *Courtesy of Laurie Bond.*

David Goode, chairman of the Norfolk Southern Corporation, was nostalgic. "We cherish this hotel. We have been proud of it. And we have loved it." Goode, like those who spoke before him, lauded the reopening as "an example of what we can do together."

Virginia Tech President Paul Torgersen cast his eye to the project's future impact as he asserted it was the most significant investment to date in directly linking education and economic development.

Later that evening, an invitation-only gala benefiting Renew Roanoke was held in the Crystal Ballroom. The sold-out event was the most jockeyed for social event of the year in the Roanoke Valley.

The reopening of the Hotel Roanoke was the result of a grander vision that culminated in the inclusion of an attached conference center. Dr. Raymond Smoot of Virginia Tech later explained the significance of the decision: "We determined, along with the city, that simply keeping the hotel open was not an option if we were to maintain its viability. The hotel was an old building that needed substantial renovation and updating, and conference facilities would have to be built alongside the hotel.... It was determined that this entire plan would cost somewhere in the neighborhood of 40–45 million dollars."

The entire project cost $43 million and involved multiple partners. As if securing the funds was not complicated enough, the financing and construction period weathered a national banking crisis coupled with a downturn in the construction funding of hotels. But the leaders of Virginia Tech and the City of Roanoke remained steadfast.

The Renew Roanoke campaign raised $5 million. Other sources included $13 million in municipal bonds, a $6 million HUD loan, $3 million from Roanoke taxpayers, $6.5 million in commercial bank loans, $4 million from the Virginia Tech Real Estate Foundation and a $1.3 million loan from the Doubletree Corporation. As costs increased and debt projections mounted, sentiment for opening the hotel complex never diminished. Bob Herbert, Roanoke's city manager at that time, said, "There were a number of times when we could have stuffed our hands in our pockets and said, 'Well, this doesn't meet financial projections' and walked away."

Herbert recalled the community support during the rebuilding phase. "One of my great memories to see what a community coming together can do when they're all pulling in the same direction and Mayor [Noel] Taylor used to say, 'You know pianos are wonderful instruments and the white keys make beautiful music, and the black keys make beautiful music, but if you can ever get all the black and white keys working together it sounds like music you've never heard.' And that's how I like to think of the hotel. Is that whole parts came together. There was never in my memory…a time that one person came publicly forward and criticized council's efforts to do this."

For all the community interest and nostalgia, however, strategic business decisions drove the process to redesign and rebuild the hotel. Herbert said he and others were haunted by the question, "If we build it, will they come?" Herbert credits the financial and leadership expertise brought to the project by Virginia Tech for driving the business model that ultimately led to the Hotel Roanoke and Conference Center's success. "The railroad was willing to give the property to Virginia Tech. Virginia Tech knew there was a recession and knew that the last thing they wanted to do was to fail reopening the project and continuing to be the owner. So to show you how smart Virginia Tech was, they negotiated a deal that if they couldn't make this work on behalf of the university financially, that it would be given back to the railroad. And of course, that was my worst nightmare that they would have to give it back to the railroad because the railroad made it clear they were not in the hotel business. Well we all worried about it a lot, but Virginia Tech made it work."

Virginia Tech was a natural and necessary partner for the project. "Virginia Tech was viewed appropriately as the entity that could generate a great deal of conferencing activity at the hotel. At the time, Tech did not have a major conference center of its own in Blacksburg, and having one in Roanoke approximate to the airport was viewed as a plus. It was viewed as an opportunity for Tech to have a first-class conferencing center. In fact, conferences literally from all over the world now come to Roanoke."

Gary Walton was hired as the general manager and oversaw the reopening of the Hotel Roanoke. Walton brought immense experience in hotel management, as the Hotel Roanoke was his thirteenth hotel. Walton initially thought his term would be short. "The longest my wife and I had been anywhere was three years. I told my wife we'd probably be here a couple of years." Walton would retire as general manager after two decades of service at Hotel Roanoke. His longevity he credited to "a combination of support from the ownership group, a great hotel and a great community."

Smoot recalled the search process for a general manager and the decision to hire Walton. "You know, one of the decisions that we had to make early on before the hotel opened was to select a general manager, and several of us traveled around the country interviewing potential general managers on their home turf of the hotel they were managing. And Gary Walton, who at the time was managing the Carolina Inn at Chapel Hill, actually came to Roanoke. We met with him here, and Gary was a young general manager at the time. He recognized the potential of the property; he recognized the attractiveness of this community and the engagement of the community in the hotel. And he came and gave great leadership. He actually arrived about two years before the hotel reopened and put together the staff."

Walton later recalled the reopening and the surprise demand for the Regency Room dining experience by locals. "Typically in a hotel you don't have that much [dining]

demand when you're first opening. But this was just slammed from day one. They were looking for the spoonbread and the peanut soup and all that, which we had. The hotel had been closed for about five years, so there was pent-up demand that we just really didn't anticipate would be as strong as it was."

The hotel's soft opening was April 3, almost a month before the official reopening marked by the dedication ceremony and gala. The soft opening with small conventions, including one with high school students, and guided tours allowed Walton and the staff to ramp up for the grand opening.

With the anticipated reopening of the Hotel Roanoke complex, Roanoke business leaders lobbied for access from the hotel to downtown. With the hotel and conference center set to attract thousands of visitors monthly, there was no easy or direct connection to Roanoke's city center of art galleries, historic farmers' market, Center in the Square, restaurants and businesses. To meet this challenge, a $2 million skywalk was constructed over the railroad tracks using state highway funds that provided the vital link.

ABOVE   The Hotel Roanoke has been an iconic structure of the Roanoke skyline since 1882. Guests today enjoy easy access to downtown via the Market Square Pedestrian Walkway. *Courtesy of Don Peterson and the* Roanoke Times.

Today, the Hotel Roanoke and Conference Center is overseen by the Hotel Roanoke Conference Center Commission (HRCCC), an entity created in March 1991 with legislation adopted by the Virginia General Assembly. Deborah Moses, who served as the commission's executive director from 1996 to July 2018, called it "a moment in time." She said both partners (the commission's members are evenly split between Virginia Tech and the City of Roanoke) faced the shared risks and the commitment to "step out" of their boxes. "It was the first time working together like this." Moses said the HRCCC "works because we work it," adding that it is a "continuing conversation" that is always evolving.

Many marriages have been launched at the Hotel Roanoke, with it playing host to numerous weddings and receptions over the years, but the greatest marriage hosted by the hotel is the one that permanently wed Virginia Tech and the City of Roanoke. That union, born by the hotel project itself, has many offspring.

"It was the first step in creating a partnership" with Virginia Tech, said Beth Doughty, executive director of the Roanoke Regional Partnership. She noted that Virginia Tech has seen the importance of the relationship and the community, in turn, understands the value of Virginia Tech.

While the HRCCC was beginning its work and the conference center was being built, another effort was getting underway. A group of business leaders in both the Roanoke and New River Valleys began to realize that the economies of the two regions were inextricably linked. Out of that epiphany grew the New Century Council, a two-year citizen effort involving some 1,100 volunteers from twelve counties and five cities. It was led by Beverly T. Fitzpatrick Jr., who was Roanoke's vice mayor and had been Dominion Bankshare Corporation's vice president for economic development and legislative affairs.

In 1995, the group issued a final report with about 150 recommendations. While some have yet to be realized, many notable suggestions came to fruition and continue to shape the region more than twenty years later. Fitzpatrick is especially proud of the Roanoke-Blacksburg Technology Council, which promotes the technology sector in the region. Its members range from small start-ups to the area's largest corporations.

The Hotel Roanoke and Conference Center continues to have long-lasting benefits for Roanoke, some of which are bricks and mortar. "Nothing was alive over there," Moses remembers of the former railroad office buildings near the hotel (Norfolk Southern having moved to a new office building in the heart of downtown Roanoke). Today, those two buildings house the Roanoke Higher Education Center and downtown apartments at 8 North Jefferson Street, known as The Crossings. Both are the result of another donation by the railroad, this time to the Roanoke Foundation for Downtown, Inc. Fitzpatrick agrees that the renewed Hotel made the two projects much easier. He was at the time a member of the foundation. "We gave the Higher Ed building to them free and clear. We sold the lower building to the Redevelopment Housing Authority that did the apartments, and we sold the [former NW passenger] station to Center in the Square to do the Link Museum."

The "crown jewel" of the Virginia Tech–Roanoke connection, says Doughty, is the Virginia Tech Carilion School of Medicine and Research Institute. Where the railroad's vision led Roanoke forward in the nineteenth and twentieth centuries, the healthcare sector has taken up that challenge in the twenty-first. Located on what was once an underused, almost brownfield stretch of Jefferson Street just south of the downtown business district, VTC (as it is known) brings together Virginia Tech's strength in basic sciences, bioinformatics and engineering and Carilion Clinic's experienced medical staff and history in medical education.

On January 3, 2007, then–Virginia Tech president Charles W. Steger, then–Carilion Clinic president and CEO Edward G. Murphy and then–Virginia governor Timothy M. Kaine announced the creation of a public-private partnership: a new medical school and research institute, the Virginia Tech Carilion School of Medicine and Research Institute. Kaine, now a U.S. senator, remembers the thinking behind the effort:

> When I was governor, one of the leading health challenges in Virginia (and especially the Roanoke region) was a dwindling healthcare workforce. So when a small group from Virginia Tech and Carilion stepped forward with an idea for a medical school and research complex in Roanoke, I was determined to make that happen. Thirteen years later, the Virginia Tech Carilion campus is illustrating how Virginia Tech–Roanoke ties can strengthen the region: well-trained physicians and nurses, healthcare for residents, thousands of jobs and Roanoke becoming a cutting-edge research hub. The Hotel Roanoke was an important precursor to what we accomplished with the Carilion project and, I believe, what Roanoke and Virginia Tech will continue to accomplish for decades to come.

The school and research institute are part of a medical campus nearly adjacent to Carilion Clinic's flagship hospital, Roanoke Memorial. They, too, are brick-and-mortar examples of what began with the Hotel Roanoke and Conference Center. As a further connection to Blacksburg, the medical school is partially constructed with Hokie Stone, the traditional stone used on the Virginia Tech campus in Blacksburg.

Like the many visionaries before her—dating back to 1882—Nancy Howell Agee, president and CEO of Carilion Clinic, understands the importance of the ongoing partnership.

What began in the '90s as an effort to save a community icon has blossomed into a fruitful partnership that today includes a medical school and research institute within a broader Virginia Tech Carilion Health Sciences and Technology Campus, and that's merely the beginning. The bold move that Carilion Clinic and Virginia Tech made in the late 2000s to combine the strengths of a top healthcare system and a top research university has further transformed and defined our region. Our partnership continues to fuel economic development and growth in the surrounding Roanoke Innovation Corridor. It isn't difficult to glimpse the exciting future ahead for a region that is investing in healthcare, science, technology and education, while embracing its roots by supporting institutions like the Hotel Roanoke.

What would Frederick Kimball think today of his railroad hotel built on a wheat field overlooking the town of Big Lick? His railroad may have largely left the city it helped found, but its influence continues. He would have a hard time wrapping his mind around the connection to Virginia Tech, which was barely ten years old when the Hotel welcomed its first guest. In 1882, Blacksburg was a long way away.

From his vision—and the vision of Roanoke and Virginia Tech leaders who were in the right place at the right time—has grown a partnership that strengthens both partners and the communities around them. "It's tough for a small-size metro area to prosper," said Doughty. Thanks to Virginia Tech's direct involvement, "our fates are intertwined. We have to make our own way and our own fun."

The Hotel opened in 1882 and reopened in 1995. So much has changed since the latter. What will the Roanoke–Virginia Tech connection yield in the next quarter century? Stay tuned!

Appendix A

HOTEL ROANOKE TIMELINE,
1880–2019

1882

OCTOBER: George L. Jacoby, hotel manager, registers first guests.
DECEMBER 25: Hotel officially opens.

1883

Big Lick changed to Roanoke and new city incorporated.
American Institute of Mining Engineers convention is Hotel's first.

1890

Addition creates sun parlor, raises room total to ninety-four.

1895

The Liberty Bell visits Hotel Roanoke.

Courtesy Virginia Room, Roanoke Public Libraries.

1898

JULY: Major fire closes hotel.

1899

JANUARY: Hotel reopens.

1916

New three-story, seventy-two-room wing added.

1931

New four-story and garage added at a cost of $225,000.

1938

Million-plus-dollar renovation puts Tudor entrance on Hotel.
Kenneth Hyde returns to Hotel as co-manager with George Denison.

1940

Chef Fred Brown invents Hotel's signature dish, peanut soup.

1943

Pine Room turned into officers' club for fliers training in Roanoke.

1947

Hyde, back from the war, oversees $1.5 million addition of new south wing.

1954

Hotel is host to Miss Virginia Pageant for first time.

1955

New wing adds Shenandoah Room, guest rooms for $1.2 million.
Fountain Room replaced by Coffee Shop.

1962

Swimming pool opens.

1963

Hotel opens Motor Hotel to meet competition.
Hotel registers 3 millionth guest, Charles Zoppa of Richmond.

1964

Mahalia Jackson, noted singer, becomes first black guest registered in the Hotel.
Three-year redecoration plans include 190 rooms, ballroom, Peacock Alley.

1967

Virginia's governor and six predecessors celebrate Hotel's eighty-fifth anniversary.
Swimming pool enclosed to permit year-round use.

1971

Regents make first appearance in Regency Room.

1974

Vice President Gerald Ford visits Hotel on political mission.

1975

Whistle Stop opens.

1977

Terrace Lounge opens off Regency Room.

1982

Governor Robb and Virginia General Assembly mark Hotel's centennial; Hotel celebrates
    further with a huge "cake" instead of a Christmas tree, special menus.
Hotel announces million-dollar refurbishing program.

1983

Passenger rail service ends in Roanoke.
Hotel employees begin strike in October.

1984

Strike ends in April, six months later.

1986

Another major redecorating program announced.

1989

Norfolk Southern gives Hotel to Virginia Tech; Regents play in Regency Room for the last
    time. Closing dinner dance held in ballroom. After flag-lowering ceremonies in front of
    hotel on November 30, the Hotel closes. Sale of Hotel contents begins on December 4,
    continues for seventeen days.

1993

Ground is broken for the new conference center adjacent to the Hotel.

Gary Walton is hired as general manager.

1995

Hotel Roanoke and Conference Center officially reopens on April 29 with a Doubletree affiliation.

Conference Center is state of the art, with fiber access to the worldwide web.

City of Roanoke opens the skywalk connecting the Hotel Roanoke to the historic City Market.

2000

Roanoke Higher Education Center opens for classes in a former Norfolk Southern office building.

2001

Hotel guestrooms and lobby renovated.

2007

Virginia Tech, Carilion Clinic and the Commonwealth of Virginia announce plans for medical school and research institute.

2007–8

125th anniversary of the Hotel. Time capsule is buried.

Major renovation of guest rooms, public space and Garden Courtyard.

Courtesy of Hotel Roanoke.

2010

Virginia Tech Carilion admits its first class.

2013

Regency Room undergoes major renovation.
Stephen Demarco is named executive chef.

2014

Major outdoor pool renovation creates lush resort-style ambiance.

2015

Hotel Roanoke celebrates twentieth anniversary of hotel reopening and opening of
    conference center.

2016

Hotel Roanoke becomes Curio Collection by Hilton.
Brian Wells is named general manager.

2017

Roanoke becomes the most southern end of the northeast corridor for Amtrak passenger rail
    service on October 30.

2018

Former president Jimmy Carter is a guest at the hotel in May.
Steam Coffee + Eatery opens in Conference Center lobby.
Hotel Roanoke and Regency Room earn AAA Four Diamond Ratings (see page 3 in the
    color section).

Courtesy of Hotel Roanoke.

HOTEL MANAGERS
George L. Jacoby (1882–88)
Fred Foster (1888–93)
S.K. Campbell (1893–1901)
Fred Foster (1901–15)
Mrs. Fred Foster (1915–22)
W.A. Dameron (1922–28)
Fay M. Thomas (1928–30)
Kenneth Hyde (1930–35)
George Denison (1935–38)
Kenneth Hyde and George Denison, co-managers (1938–63)
George Denison (1963–64)
Carl Thurston (1963–69)
Fred Walker (1969–71)
Ken Wilkey (1971–76)
Janet Jenkins (1976–80)
Peter Kipp (1980–86)
Doreen Hamilton Fishwick (1986–89)
Gary Walton (1993–2016)
Brian Wells (2016–present)

PEANUT SOUP AND SPOONBREAD

HOTEL ROANOKE PEANUT SOUP

¼ pound butter
1 small onion (diced)
2 branches celery (diced)
3 tablespoons flour
2 quarts chicken broth
1 pint peanut butter
⅓ teaspoon celery salt
1 teaspoon salt
1 tablespoon lemon juice
½ cup ground peanuts

Melt butter in cooking vessel and add onion and celery. Sauté for 5 minutes (not brown). Add flour and mix well. Add hot chicken broth and cook for a half hour. Remove from stove, strain and add peanut butter, celery salt, salt and lemon juice. Sprinkle ground peanuts on soup just before serving. Serves 10.

Appendix B

HOTEL ROANOKE SPOONBREAD

1½ cups cornmeal
1⅓ teaspoons salt
1 teaspoon sugar
1½ cups boiling water
⅛ pound butter
5 eggs
2 cups milk
1 teaspoon baking powder

Mix cornmeal, salt and sugar together and scald with boiling water. Add melted butter. Beat eggs and add milk to eggs. Combine two mixtures and add baking powder. Pour into baking pan and bake 30 to 40 minutes at 350 degrees. Serves 10.

ABOUT THE AUTHORS

The late DONLAN PIEDMONT had a distinguished career in communications that included being the Norfolk Southern Corporation's national public relations director, from which he retired. He passed away in 2005.

LISA FENDERSON is a media content consultant and an executive producer and host at Blue Ridge PBS. She produced the companion video to this book, *Hotel Roanoke: The Grand Old Lady on the Hill*, in 2019.

NELSON HARRIS, a local historian and author of over a dozen books on the region's history, is a minister and former mayor of the city of Roanoke.

ANNE PIEDMONT, daughter of Donlan, is an accomplished writer and has been a marketing and economic development professional in the Roanoke Valley for over thirty years.

Visit us at
www.historypress.com